BALD, FAT & CRAZY

BALD, FAT & CRAZY

How I Beat Cancer While Pregnant
with One Daughter and Adopting Another

STEPHANIE HOSFORD

NOTHING BUT THE TRUTH, LLC

SAN FRANCISCO

Published in 2015 by Nothing But The Truth, LLC
NothingButtheTruth.com
Nothing But The Truth name and logo are trademarks of Nothing But The Truth Publishing, LLC.

Printed in the United States of America
First Edition

Editing by Sam Barry
Cover design by theBookDesigners
Text design and ebook design by ALL Publications

Library of Congress Control Number: 2015903369

ISBN: 978-0-9904652-7-0 (paperback)
ISBN: 978-0-9904652-8-7 (hardcover)
ISBN: 978-0-9904652-9-4 (ePub ebook)

For Cancer, because you lost. Get used to it.

PROLOGUE

October 2012
"Soul Meets Body" – Death Cab for Cutie

"Is it just me, or are these difficult for everyone?" I ask, fumbling with the cloth straps of my blue snowflake print hospital gown. "And who thought to call them *gowns*? Am I supposed to feel glamorous in this?" I glance over at my husband, Grant, to see if he's listening to me. He looks up from his phone and grins. He heard me. He knows, we both know, that my rant stems from being extra nervous today and that the only answers I'm truly looking for are in other parts of this hospital, namely Radiology and The Lab. "Plus, I'm freezing." I shiver for effect.

Grant stands up and opens his arms. "You okay?" he asks. I move in for a hug, probably my eighth from him this morning, each one propping me up for about 30 minutes until I need another.

"Yeah, I'm okay," I say into his chest, hoping it's true.

"It's going to be fine, you know," he says. No, I don't know, but I refrain from stating this aloud. I'm trying to keep it positive, but without being so overconfident that I assume the cancer would never come back. It's not wise to challenge cancer, especially at your five-year checkup.

"Okay," I say.

We let go and Grant sits back down to return to his phone. I continue my struggle with the shapeless cotton garment. I cross the right portion over the left only to reopen it and wrap the left side over the right instead. I am determined to make sense of the many ties and pair them up in the correct way so that no section of my torso is exposed to the elements. At least it's not one of those weird, stiff paper robes with the slick plastic belts. Those are impossible.

"You think I'd be used to these by now," I say, making my final adjustments.

I climb up onto the exam table and sit down. The smooth, white paper crinkles beneath me as I shift my weight from one sit bone to the other a few times and then lean back, placing my head against the small pillow. I take a deep breath—in through the nose, out through the mouth—in an attempt to relax.

I'm glad I remembered to bring socks. I don't know if it's due to nerves or the fact that I'm essentially naked in here, but my toes are always numb with cold and turn an eerie bluish-purplish color for these appointments. I had to resort to my Christmas pair, though, because all the regular ones are in the overflowing laundry basket at home. I really don't like socks with anything at all printed on them, except maybe the words 'Dri-Fit' or the decidedly helpful 'L' or 'R'. Now I have candy canes on my feet. And it's October. I used to be more pulled together than this.

Maybe I should dry my sweaty palms with an automated squirt of hand sanitizer. I look at the dispenser stuck to the wall. But I know I'll sniff my hands after rubbing them together, and it will only make me more anxious, catapulting me back to the sterile environs of the Infusion Center and the hours I spent in there getting pumped full of toxins. I hope this olfactory association doesn't continue forever because the clean scent of Purell is really not a bad one.

"This is it," I announce to Grant, who is more than aware

of the significance of today's test results. "This is the big one," I continue, "the moment of truth."

"I know, Bug," Grant responds, smiling at me and reaching for my hand.

I rub my palm back and forth on my robe to dry it off before accepting his offer. He gives it a comforting squeeze and keeps holding it, his other hand free to continue checking for work messages.

"It's going to be fine," he says again.

I nod and close my eyes. I need to relax. I need my mind to leave this room for a while. Okay, here we go. I'm reclined in a beach chair instead of on this exam table. I'm looking out onto a serene blue ocean. I can hear the waves crashing, the seagulls crooning overhead. My body is completely free of disease.

Aaahh, that's better. I feel so loose, so unencumbered, so…nope, I can't. As much as I want, I can't stay here at the beach. Not today. I open my eyes and reenter the room. I can't shake the superstition that fate might laugh in my face again if I allow myself to become too convinced of wellness. It might be irrational, but I can't take the risk.

Instead, I take another deep breath and survey my surroundings. On my right is the wide, mauve door that is closed for our privacy. I hear the familiar voices of the nurse practitioners, RNs, aides and doctors on the other side of it. Their muffled conversations and footsteps grow louder as they pass by my room, tapering off as they head further down the hallway. If I were to listen closely I would hear words like "IV drip" and "port," but I don't care to, so I alternate between clearing my throat and whistling a made up melody to drown them out. Okay, not really helping and now my throat hurts. I should have brought my iPod.

Normally, Grant and I would be chatting with each other, viewing any opportunity to be alone out of the house together as a date. But there is nothing normal about this day.

I return to room surveillance, anything to distract me from the imminent meeting with Dr. Sung, my oncologist. I start with the heavy, grey curtain just inside the doorway, the bulk of which hangs at my feet. My eyes follow the curtain upward to the semi-circular curve of its metal track on the ceiling. I look across the room, scan the counter-top, the cabinets above it and the drawers below it, all the same smooth mauve as the door. Actually, do I hear the door unlatching? I give it a sideways glance as my stomach clenches. No, no one yet. Stomach not unclenching though. I hate this.

I shift my gaze further left and review the laminated posters pinned to the wall. One lists the "Patient Rights and Responsibilities." The other features the "Pain Measurement Scale," with numbers ranging 0-10 and corresponding circular faces printed underneath. The first face presents a smile and the last bears an expression of sheer anguish. Yikes.

Behind Grant is a small desk sticking out from the wall, a computer monitor hung above it. The seat of Dr. Sung's swivel chair is pushed under the desk, the back pressed up to the edge. I'm running out of objects to focus on in this generic exam room.

I sit up straight, cross my dangling ankles, and stretch my legs out in front of me. Can it be October already? We've been so busy and time has flown by—except for lately whenever I've thought of this moment. Then it stood still. And now here I am, feeling slightly nauseated, waiting for the outcome of my chest x-ray and blood work.

I look down at my arm, the middle portion still wrapped in neon green self-adhesive dressing. Now there's an activity. I can peel that off slowly until I reach the underlying cotton ball and then throw them both away. I start to hum Maroon 5's "Payphone" as I work on the bandage. "Where have the times gone, baby it's all wrong...hmm, hmm, hmm." The music helps divert my attention more than the hospital room. Thank you, Adam Levine.

I'm grateful to all those songs really, the ones that made me feel powerful and in control of my situation, even when I wasn't. Some were so angry, like "Killing in the Name" from Rage Against The Machine, others mellower, like The All-American Rejects' "Move Along," but each hand-picked by me for one reason or another—sometimes for its lyrics, other times for its beat or even simply its title. Musically speaking, I'm hoping for a Flo Rida "Club Can't Even Handle Me" type of day rather than one dominated by "Here It Goes Again" by Ok Go. I can hear them both, though, competing for my future. Another deep inhale through the nose.

Grant reaches for my hand again as Dr. Sung bursts through the door.

I hold my breath.

CHAPTER 1

September 2007
"Get the Party Started" – Pink

"We should go to this reunion, right?" I ask Sara, my best friend from high school, as we trot along on the YMCA treadmills. I pull my right earbud out so I can converse but not lose Eminem's "Without Me" completely. It's taking me a while to warm up in the overly air conditioned gym this morning. I prefer to jog outside, but it's nearly 100 degrees today, dangerously hot for our usual three-mile loop around the Rose Bowl. I hope Ethan is taking it easy on the playground this morning. Did I put the sweat-proof sunscreen on him or just the regular one?

"We did miss the ten-year."

"Hmm? Ten-year what?" I ask, preoccupied by the thought of my son's potentially pink face. Did I remember to slather his arms and the back of his neck?

"Reunion. We missed our ten-year reunion," Sara says, not even slightly out of breath despite far outpacing me. She's a natural runner, as the track coaches back in high school so often said. It could be she's even faster now that she chases her three kids around for a good portion of the day. Or maybe I have gotten slower. It's hard to say. I never ran track. I was too busy deciding which member of Duran Duran I liked most and wondering if I was popular. I am still waiting for my natural abilities to reveal themselves, aside from a knack for being easily distracted during conversations. Lately, I feel as though I have a gift for choosing just the right emoticon to convey tone in my texts, too. Can't forget that.

"Oh, I know. So we're, like, totally going to this one!" I respond, attempting to impersonate my high school voice, which really is not as far from my adult voice as it should be.

I then conjure up a favorite ideal image of myself—one I've strived for and failed to achieve over the years—one in which I am overwhelmingly svelte and fashionable, impressing others with my cool confidence and sharp wit.

But this time will be different, I tell myself. This time I will really follow through with the plan. I will shun carbs and sugar! I will exercise even more aggressively and do Pilates! I will have a predetermined outfit and well-rehearsed hairstyle. High school was not my *worst* era, looks-wise—that was junior high (thanks to home perms, braces and fashion sense inspired by Sarah Jessica Parker... in *Square Pegs*), but it certainly wasn't my best, so I'm striving to make a better impression this time. And by that, I mean I want to look great. And if I look great, I reason, then the confidence will follow, and along with that, the wit. It's not that I need a spot on *Extreme Makeover*, but as I am closer to 40 years old than 30, it's going to require some strategy.

Luckily, the event is a whole year away—plenty of time for my Reunion Plan 2008 to be pulled together. I can almost hear my fellow 1988 classmates whispering to each other words of approval as I pass by. Oh, and this tall, handsome, Ethan Hawke look-alike holding my hand? Yes, he's my husband, Grant. At least that part is already true...

"You're right," Sara says, bringing me back to the present setting once again. "We should go."

"Cool!" I stick the bud back in my ear and turn the iPod's

volume up. I increase my jog pace to prove to myself my commitment. Now it's playing Kanye West's "Stronger." Perfect.

Two days later, we are back on the treadmills as the heat outside continues its oppression. I bring up a new topic, one that has nothing to do with the reunion or my recent obsession regarding how to handle the laugh lines that seem to multiply daily around my eyes. "So, um, last night, I found a small lump in my left boob," I reveal to Sara, "I felt it while I was in bed giving them both a squeeze. They've been sore and I wanted to check their status, you know?" My hands move instinctively up to my breasts as I tell her this.

"I'm sure it's nothing," Sara waves her hand dismissively, "probably your period. Mine get sore and lumpy every month and then it all goes away." Phew. Sara doesn't get worked up over most things, with the exception of anything related to her boobs. Breast cancer runs in her family, so she is on continuous high alert, scheduling extra mammograms and MRI's to keep on top of things. I'll take her nonchalant assessment of my issue as a good sign. And I should probably remove my hands from my breasts, I realize as I look down.

It's still there. I want to ignore it, but my fingers keep reaching for that spot. I need to call my OB/GYN so that he can tell me it's nothing, just my period, and that it will shrink away, just like Sara said it would. Or maybe it's like the time seven years ago when I had a small fibrous cyst excised from my left breast. It was absolutely benign and left behind only the teeniest white line of a scar on my skin.

But still, *nothing* to worry about. Or perhaps it's more like that fluid filled cyst five years ago that I discovered while adjusting my bikini top on a beach in Oahu. That hadn't posed a threat either, so I am nearly completely certain this one is equally harmless.

A couple of days later, I sit reading *Sunset* magazine in my gynecologist's waiting area, attempting to commit to memory a recipe for a 'guiltless' dessert. I bet if I ripped the page slowly out, no one would hear it…I can't. Too delinquent.

I look around the room at the other patients. Most of them are visibly expecting, clad in maternity tank tops or sundresses. I remember my frequent stops at the store, A Pea in the Pod, when I was pregnant with Ethan. It was the only time in my adult life I actually hoped to fit into the next bigger size with each visit. My heart has been eager for a second baby for the past four years, but apparently my uterus has not. And although I am thrilled that we are only a couple of months away from completing an international adoption, being surrounded by these round bellies in various states of prominence, I can't deny the longing to wear those maternity clothes again.

Well, at least I can get up off this sofa without assistance and I don't have to pee every eight seconds. With that in mind, I stand up quickly and hustle across the room to return the magazine to its original table, bending over with ease to pick up a fallen pamphlet on birth control along the way. Jealous of this agility, anyone?

No one is looking at me. I sigh and head back to my spot on the couch.

Rather than dwell further on my reproductive failures, I begin to form a plan for the rest of the day after my escape from this office.

I would like to get in some exercise before picking up Ethan from kindergarten. On our way home, I could make a surprise detour to his favorite restaurant, where we can share spicy tuna rolls and salty edamame. I knew introducing a five year old to sushi could be expensive. And it is. But I pay because I finally found something that my Daddy's Boy considers cool and associates with me rather than Grant. It's now become our thing, Ethan and I, just the two of us, and I smile, imagining his excitement as we pull into the restaurant parking lot and he begins his plea for the 'Premium Rolls.' I'm sure I'll be talked into one with the word 'Spider' or 'Dynamite' in it and he'll write the 'r' on the paper menu using the undersized yellow eraser-less pencil.

Then he will begin his enthusiastic, rapid-fire status updates about school. We'll we sit in our usual booth toward the back of the small restaurant. And since Ethan is a member of the 'every good story deserves embellishment' club, his account should take us all the way through the meal and maybe even frozen yogurt.

A nurse opens the door halfway, pokes her head out and calls me in for my appointment. I don't bother to change into a gown, figuring I can save some time by simply lifting up my tank top and jog bra for this brief visit.

"It's right up here," I describe to Dr. Hogan as soon as he steps into the room. I put my fingertips directly on the lump. Damn, it's still there, a hard chickpea-sized annoyance.

"Hmmm," I hear as he steps closer to perform a professional feel. My breasts are still sore and I'm reminded of this as he palpates them. There's no point in mentioning it though because my period should be here any minute and it will cease to be an issue.

"Let's send you for a mammogram."

"Oh…okay." Darn. Another annoying disruption to my schedule, but I know I'll follow through because now it's a loose end and I generally feel obligated to tie those up.

"It's probably nothing, but let's just be sure so we can put your mind at ease, alright?"

"Sure, um, but can I go to the Radiology that's upstairs rather than the other one?" I would prefer to avoid the place where my miscarriage was confirmed two years ago. Does Dr. Hogan remember that? I search his inscrutable face for evidence of recollection. Nothing.

It was he who sent me there that morning after searching in vain for a fetal heartbeat. It was in this very room, too. I cast my gaze downward, remembering the impossibly dark, still image on the ultrasound screen. I'll never forget the feeling that my heart stopped, too, that day, when I realized my pregnancy was over. Just like that. Over.

"No problem," he obliges as he scribbles out the referral. Good, it's time to go. I pull my shirt back down and head for the exit.

After a quick workout, and then sushi, yogurt and the latest installment of Ethan's Tales from the Playground, I call the hospital to make my appointment. I notice that the slip of paper in my hand has two options—'Diagnostic' and 'Routine,' and that 'Diagnostic' is the box that has been checked. Why is that? What is there to diagnose? Seriously, I just ran four miles today. If I were sick, wouldn't I feel different?

"Does your referral say Diagnostic or Routine?"

"Oh, uh, it's Diagnostic," I answer the scheduler, but then feel compelled to add, "You know, my doctor just wants to set my mind at ease. He said that."

"Okay, can you come in tomorrow at 11:00?"

I look at the calendar stuck to the refrigerator door by a heart-shaped ceramic magnet. 'Thumbody loves you' is scrawled over an indented print of Ethan's 4-year old thumb. "That will work," I say, jotting it down in the small square that contains 'Ethan's soccer practice—4:00.'

"So we'll see you tomorrow in Radiology at 11:00."

"I have to go to for a mammogram tomorrow morning," I tell my mom and Grant at dinner a couple of hours later.

"You do? Why?" Grant asks.

"Oh, that dumb little lump is still there and Dr. Hogan wants me to have it checked. It's probably like what I had a few years ago, remember?" I stand up to clear the dinner dishes. Ethan is rolling around with Rio, our lovable lab, in the living room. Those two have similar qualities, I've always thought—my blonde, strong, good-hearted boys.

"Do you want me to go with you?" Grant asks.

"I'll go with you," my mom offers, too.

"No, no. It's nothing. Just routine," I turn away from everyone so they can't see the tension in my facial expression. "I'll be fine."

"Let me take you, Steph," Mom persists.

"*No*, Mom. I am fine. Seriously. It's just *routine*." I really do feel okay, at least 98% okay, but it's that squirrelly 2% that sometimes involuntarily appears on my face, so I force a smile to override that, hopefully sparing us all from further debate.

The next morning I am in a hospital gown, telling the technician about my reason for being here. She feels around with her fingers and then marks the spot with a little sticker.

The letters 'BB' are printed on it. Maybe it stands for 'Bad Booby'? It should, considering the time and 2% of okayness it has already cost me.

I am impressed that the tech is able to get my small B minus cup between the glass plates of the mammography machine in the first place. I have to control my giggling when I look down at my flattened, pale boob. It reminds me of a jellyfish, minus the tentacles and graceful movement. I'm just as sore as yesterday, if not more, so the humor of my situation is fleeting. My left breast is x-rayed several times at various angles as I focus on the wall in front of me and try to hold still.

The lump does indeed show itself on the mammography film and the tech tells me she is going to have the radiologist look at it more closely. I am free to leave, though, so I head back into the small dressing room. I'm glad Mom didn't accompany me here because she'd already be stressed, probably pelting the tech with questions about what this could all mean, imparting a story to me about a random friend and the results of a semi-related medical procedure.

"You know Lois?" she'd ask. I'd nod, though not really recalling this person and not interested enough to dig through my mental list of Mom's Contacts Twice Removed to do anything about it.

"Well, her daughter-in-law, you know, the one who sings, and has the son who's hyperactive?"

"Uh-huh," I'd respond, my mind already wandering.

"Well, she had an MRI last year and they told her…"

But mostly she'd worry and neither of us needs that. Hopefully, I'll get my call from Dr. Hogan within a few days to let me know everything is fine and it will cease to be a topic of conversation at all.

Later that afternoon, Ethan is seated at the kitchen table with me leaning over him as we go over his homework packet. The phone rings, interrupting our review of the letter 'B.' I answer and it is someone from Radiology. Already? I am asked to come back that afternoon so that the doctor can perform an ultrasound on the "mass." Mass? Why is it being referred to as a 'mass' all of a sudden? It sounds so…*alive.*

But I can't come in today because Ethan has soccer practice and I can't put his future scholarship to UCLA in jeopardy by missing it. We set my return appointment for tomorrow morning. I know Mom will want to come for sure. I'm planning to say no.

"Guess what?" I ask Grant as we are getting into bed later that evening. "I get to go into Radiology again tomorrow and get an ultrasound on this thing." I tell him as I feel the stubborn, intrusive pebble.

"Oh, yeah, how did that go? I forgot to ask you. They want you to come back? Should I go with you?"

"No, you don't need to come with me," I answer him. "It's probably with Dr. Wilson, though. Remember the one that confirmed the miscarriage?" My voice catches a little.

"I do. Sorry, hon," Grant says, rubbing my shoulder. "You're sure you don't want me to come with you?"

I sort of do now, but I also don't want him to have to miss work for this. Work should be missed for fun stuff like road trips to Santa Barbara, stopping along the way at the outlet mall in Camarillo to shop for boots. Not that Grant wears boots. That might be more why I would miss work. Not that I have a job.

His furrowed brow and two offers to accompany me are making me nervous now, though, because Grant is not a worrier. I handle the worry in this family, having both the genetics and the upbringing to allow for this impressive skill.

"No, no. I'll be fine," I say, trying really hard to convince us both of this and impress him with my strictly positive attitude. But why is it starting to remind me of when we were first dating and I told Grant I liked to camp outdoors?

The next day, Dr. Wilson walks into the exam room with a nurse in tow. Her large glasses and friendly smile are just as I remember. I do recall her being sweet and comforting on that sad morning two years ago, but I don't bring up our past because I can't think of a reason why I should.

"Good morning," she says, walking toward the ultrasound machine, which is whirring softly beside me as I lay on the table in my hospital gown, opening in the front. I expose my left breast and she puts the probe onto it, directly onto the 'mass' and looks at the screen. I look, too. There it is, a black amorphous blob against a somewhat mottled white background. It appears to undulate as the probe is shifted around. I look to Dr. Wilson. Her eyes have narrowed and her brow is beginning to furrow as she tilts her head to one side and then the other, focusing her gaze on the image in front of her.

"I'd like to do a core needle biopsy."

"Oh, okay." Did she say 'needle'?

The next morning Grant and I are back in Radiology. It's been scarcely 24 hours and I am back on the same exam table in a hospital gown, the ultrasound machine still humming next to me. Today there is an added feature, though. A small metal stand is next to the machine with a frighteningly large syringe resting on a surgical napkin. Dr. Wilson comes in, a friendly looking female technician close behind her, and walks over to the sink to wash her hands.

"Hello again."

"Good morning," Grant responds from his chair near the foot of the examination table.

"Hi," I say, glance at the needle and take a deep inhale. Dr. Wilson is then at my side, picking up the instrument.

"I'm going to get a few samples of the tissue we saw yesterday with this, and then we'll send them off to the lab for analysis, okay?"

"Okay." I raise my eyebrows and realize this syringe is much bigger and thicker than any I have personally dealt with and is in fact beginning to look more like a bicycle pump. I bite my lip and look at Grant who gives me a reassuring squeeze on my foot.

I accept an offer of topical numbing cream, and shortly thereafter the technician places the lubed ultrasound probe onto my breast and holds it there while Dr. Wilson pierces my skin with the syringe. This is surprisingly not painful and I am impressed with my grit. It is short-lived.

"OW!" I blurt out as Dr. Wilson pushes some sort of button on the instrument causing the needle to punch into the dark mass displayed on the screen and grab a sample of it.

"I'm sorry, honey," she offers, keeping her eyes on the image, "but I have to get a few more of those for the lab."

"It's alright," I lie, and then endure about eight more assaults, each one sounding like the *thunk* of a firing nail gun. "So this is probably just a cyst, right?" I inquire of Dr. Wilson as she mercifully extracts the syringe from my chest.

"Well, I couldn't tell for sure from the ultrasound, but the borders look irregular in a few places?" She points to the screen that is still displaying my tissues.

"But cysts can do that sometimes. It's just hard to know exactly what it is until the lab looks at the samples." Dr. Wilson places a large Band-Aid on the point of needle entry.

"I'll call you as soon as I know anything. Now take it easy today."

"Can I go to taekwondo tonight?"

"Probably not," Grant answers first and gives me his 'aren't you paying attention?' look.

"Um, no," Dr. Wilson confirms, handing me an ice pack.

But I am in love with my new martial arts obsession so this is disappointing, and I glumly imagine my black belt (which is only 12 belts away) slip further from my grasp.

CHAPTER 2

"Pinch Me" – Barenaked Ladies

It's Friday. Mom and I sit outside on the back patio of a local cafe, our round wrought-iron table shaded by a large umbrella. A warm, jasmine-scented breeze gently wafts through the air. I inhale deeply. For once, I am not in workout clothes during this hour of the day. I look again at my cell phone resting quietly on the table near my plate. Where is that call from Dr. Wilson?

"This place is so quaint," Mom says, using one of her adjectives that no one else ever does.

"Simply charming," I respond with a faux British accent, happy to redirect my attention from the phone.

"Oh stop," she says, playfully hitting my arm. "You just love making fun of me." I grin at her.

It's been two years since Dad died and I can tell that Mom has arrived at a better place, the dark cloud of grief finally lifted. Time plus professional counseling were key factors in her recovery. Currently, Grant, Ethan and I live with her in the house where I grew up, allowing us to save money for a down payment on a home of our own in this pricey neighborhood. I would never have thought I'd end up back in my hometown. Sometimes the mazelike, convoluted routes we think we're taking in life end up being circles.

As a teenager, I couldn't wait to escape what I considered to be the most stiflingly boring town in the universe. Why couldn't we live closer to the beach or in the valley where things actually happened or at least seemed to in movies like *Valley Girl* and *Less Than Zero*? My plan was to leave and only return now and then for short visits, and maybe a little longer in the summer when I could swim in our pool.

For nearly fifteen years, my plan worked splendidly. It began after high school when I happily took off to UC Santa Barbara where I spent four years studying on the beach or working on my tan atop the Pi Beta Phi sorority house sun deck. Next, while most of my college friends moved to San Diego or Manhattan Beach, I headed to Boston for graduate school, where I truly loved that first snow, and even the second and third. But when it was still snowing in April, I knew that not even J.P. Licks ice cream on Newbury Street could keep me there beyond graduation.

I met Grant while in Boston and we'd been dating only six months when he was offered a job in São Paulo, Brazil. He asked me to come with him, and I agreed, a decision that made my parents, especially Mom, significantly irritated.

"Brazil??" she challenged. "Why in the world would you want to live there? And you're not even engaged." That was the real problem for her, I knew, the lack of a ring on my finger.

"Oh, I'm going," I shot back at her, arms crossed, trying desperately not to show how much I did indeed want her approval. "And I don't need any ring," I assured her, shaking my head.

Two years later, wedding band securely on my finger for over a year and having had all sorts of adventures in Brazil and Argentina (including getting engaged atop Pão de Açúcar in Rio de Janeiro—totally worth the wait and Mom's restlessness), Grant and I moved to Seattle where we ended up staying for five years. Seattle is a wonderful city, and the home of my wonderful in-laws...but (and I know this is not breaking news), it's also damp and gray a good portion of the year. I missed my flip-flops. But much more than that, I really missed my sister, Jenn. We vowed long ago to raise our kids near each other, and it was time to make that happen.

So, after a long time of living away, I have returned to La Cañada, the same sleepy yet warm suburb of my youth. I'm sure in about ten years Ethan will complain to me about the monotony of his life here, and I will understand. I will encourage him to explore the world as I did and have some adventures of his own. But until then, he will bond and play with his cousins. We can walk to school together with only a handful of cars passing by. I will run into no fewer than three friends when we shop at Trader Joe's, and we will attend the annual Fiesta Days Parade as local bands and business owners travel down Foothill Boulevard waving at everybody they know, which is everybody. I assume living near Mom will include somewhat unlimited free baby-sitting; at least that's what I inferred when she urged us to move down here. It's all coming together and I can't help but sigh with satisfaction at how my life is going.

My cell phone vibrates on the table just as the waitress places my plate down in front of me. "Hello?"

"Hello, Stephanie?"

"Yes…" I say and mouth a 'thank you' to the waitress.

"This is Dr. Hogan's office. I just want to let you know that you've been scheduled for a surgical consult on Monday at 11:00 with Dr. Conle."

That's weird. Dr. Conle? Who's that?

"I don't need a surgical consult," I tell the receptionist, confused, assuming she misdialed…but then again, she did know my name. Why would they schedule a consult on their own? I haven't even decided if I *want* this odd cyst out just now, as it would get in the way of my workouts. I'm simply waiting to be told that everything is fine.

"Please cancel it."

"Oh, okay, I'll tell Dr. Hogan that you'll reschedule on your own then?"

"Um, sure."

I have no intention of scheduling anything at the moment. I just want to eat lunch. We hang up, allowing my focus to return to curried chicken salad, delightfully yellow and full of raisins.

"Who was that?" Mom leans toward me, using her quiet voice. I'm sure this is so that we don't attract any attention to ourselves. Mom has always been a strong believer in keeping our personal/family affairs tightly under wraps, unless of course that affair sheds us in a favorable light, like when I was accepted into graduate school or when Grant and I finally got respectfully engaged. That sort of news deserves a loud voice that has every chance of being overheard.

"Oh, nothing." *Strange, though.* "Just a miscommunication."

About an hour later we pull into our driveway, Ethan in the back seat of Mom's Acura, when my phone buzzes again. This time it's Dr. Wilson.

"Oh, hi, Doctor." I'm glad to get this settled at last.

"Stephanie. Sweetie, I'm afraid that the news is not something we wanted."

No, her line was supposed to be, "Stephanie. The lump is nothing. Have a great weekend." And then I thank her for her time and wish her the same. But instead she said what she said.

"What do you mean?"

"I'm sorry, but it's a type of cancer."

What? I must have misheard that last word. I know it can't be, but it sounded a lot like ca—

"You're kidding. That's not true." comes out of my mouth before I can stop it. My brain implores me to consider that she is the worst and meanest doctor in the universe with an evil sense of humor. Why is she so mean?

"I wouldn't joke about this."

"So…you're telling me I have breast cancer?" I'm barely able to utter the words "I" and "breast cancer" in the same sentence, as they certainly do not belong anywhere near each other.

"I'm afraid so."

I intend to respond with another, "You're kidding" coupled this time with "You're a *fucking* liar," but I can't because there is no air for me to breathe, thus rendering me speechless. Where is the *air*? Is this how it feels to drown? Everything is in slow motion, except for the frenzied list my mind is assembling for me of reasons why this *cannot* be happening: I'm only 37 years old. I exercise. I eat well. I don't smoke or drink alcohol. Okay, I do drink alcohol but not *that* much, not enough to cause something like this to happen! Breast cancer does not run in my family. What the hell is going on? This doesn't make any sense!

It does make sense now, though, why that reception-ist called about the surgical consult. Dr. Hogan knew of my bad news before I did and set up the appointment. Dr. Wilson is still on the phone.

"I don't know what to do," I squeak out, and start to cry. "What do I DO?"

"You have an appointment for Monday with the surgeon on your insurance plan."

"But I *canceled* it!" My hands shake as I try to hold on to the phone.

"I'll talk to them and set it up again."

"Okay." I hang up. I cry harder, and then remember that Ethan and Mom are in the car. They just heard all of that.

I turn to look at Ethan in the back seat holding his skull and crossbones backpack in his lap. His expression is filled with fear and I want to hug and comfort him, but I can't. I can actually feel my heart breaking in my chest. I turn back around. I can't look at his precious, confused face because I think it would end me right here. I've got to pull it together or get out of this car.

Mom is being uncharacteristically silent, which scares me even more. No opinions or advice from my mom? Why is she so quiet? Is my situation unsolvable?

I mumble something about needing to go make some calls and I make a break for the house. But what calls am I supposed to be making? I can't think. I drop to my knees in the entryway, unable to move. Finally, I manage to press 1 on my speed dial for Grant's cell phone. He says hello and my throat constricts, but I somehow manage to tell him to come home immediately because I have cancer.

"You what?"

"I have c...ca...cancer. Breast cancer." I let out a strange sound, a mix between a sob and a gasp. I close my eyes tightly.

"Uh...okay. Uh, let me wrap up here and I'll come home."

"Wrap up? What could you have to wrap up?? Just leave!"

"Steph, I'm out to lunch with my boss."

"Don't tell him!"

"Uh...um, okay. Okay, honey. I'll be there as soon as I can."

I amble down the hallway into our bedroom, close the door and slowly collapse again onto the carpet. I curl up on my side into a ball, hugging my knees. I am caught in a cyclone of thoughts and unanswerable questions, being pelted by disturbing visions of my future.

What does this mean? Am I going to die? This can't be happening. My father died from cancer two years ago. It was a very rare type that affects only a few people each year. It was virulent and horrible and I watched him wither away before my eyes and then held his atrophied hand as he left this world. Is that what will happen to me now? Is it my turn to lie in that bed, the hospice nurse attempting to make me more comfortable as my family watches helplessly from the hallway?

How is this possible? How can my mother be expected to endure this? And Grant and Ethan? And my sister? How can this be? Is Ethan going to be 'that poor kid with no mommy' now?

And how about the adoption we happen to be in the middle of? What's to become of that? We have been waiting two years to be matched with a little girl in China. I have been desperately longing for her. Have I let her down, too?

The guilt is crushing.

And then suddenly the cyclone releases me and withdraws.

There's been a mistake! Clearly, my tissue samples have been misread or maybe mixed up with someone else's. That poor person; I should feel sorry for her, but mostly I just feel relieved about myself.

I sit up, wipe my nose on my sleeve and look at my red-rimmed eyes in the mirrored closet door. I finally can take a deep breath, knowing they will call on Monday and this will all be straightened out…

Grant arrives home within a minute or so. Or has it been an hour? It's impossible to know, as time appears to have stopped. My delusion of wellness dissipates when I see him in the entryway, tossing his workbag onto the floor and walking toward me. The reality of his tight hug reawakens the storm and I begin to whimper and then wail effusively against his chest. In between my muffled sobs, I hear his voice.

"You're the strongest woman I know. It's going to be fine."

How can he say that? He is insane. Can't he see that I am weak and ruined? I am a helpless blob.

After a number of minutes, I lift my head off of Grant's saturated shirt.

"I need to tell Jenn."

"Okay, should we drive over?"

He knows this is not the type of news I want to tell my one and only sibling on the phone, even if she didn't live seven minutes away.

"Yes," I sniff, "but first I want to find Ethan."

I gently open the door to my mom's bedroom and there they are at her desk, Ethan on Mom's lap, playing a game on the computer. They both look over at me.

"Hi, Mommy."

"Hi, honey."

My bottom lip quivers. I don't know what to tell him at the moment, so I walk over, kneel down, pull his head to my chest and kiss his hair. "Mommy's okay," I hear myself whisper. Isn't that what a responsible parent should say? Or is it the worst thing to do, to lie to him like that? I don't know. I know nothing anymore. My brain has been cleared of all answers since that phone call from Dr. Wilson. When I stand up, my mom stands, too, placing Ethan on the chair alone to continue his game. *Please don't cry, Mom.* I brace myself for the onslaught of tears we are about to share.

But then my mother, my fiercely protective and historically emotional mother, takes my hand, looks me in the eye and says, "You're going to fight this. And you're going to be fine." I look down at the carpet, take a deep and shaky breath, and lift my gaze back up to her. My mom is still looking right at me, but *not* crying.

Oh, I get it…so she's crazy, too, then, along with my husband.

Grant and I leave for my sister's house. I'm not sure how I'm going to break the news. Usually I'm too late to brief her on anything because Mom has already told her. But I know that won't be the case this afternoon.

I have no doubt I am psychically connected to my sister, even though we're not twins and I don't believe in psychics. But there have been several occurrences in my life that cannot be explained any other way.

For example, when Grant and I learned that I was about four and a half weeks pregnant with Ethan we told no one, deciding to keep our exciting secret to ourselves for a few days before sharing it with our families. Jenn arrived from California the next day for a visit, put her hand on my belly and said with a knowing grin, "Do you have something to tell me?"

It is not a big surprise to me then that as we drive onto her street a few minutes later she is already walking outside to meet me, somehow knowing the news I am about to share with her. No words are exchanged, just hugs and the onset of a new round of sobbing by me.

"It's going to be fine," she assures me, squeezing me tighter. Is everyone on Team Crazy around here? Or is this just what they are supposed to say, that I'm 'going to be fine'? What does that even mean? I guess it's better than my family breaking down with me because then I'd be utterly lost. But what is *fine*? It's only been three hours since Dr. Wilson told me I have cancer and I already can't remember what it was like to be fine.

Back at home I call my friend Sara and tell her the news, my voice cracking as I reveal the outcome of what we agreed a few days ago would be nothing.

"Oh shit, Steph, that was supposed to be me. It's *my* family with the cancer history."

"I know, right? The irony." I sniff, and force out a slight laugh that goes nowhere beyond an exasperated exhale. And although I would never wish this on my friend, I truly *don't* understand how I can be the one with cancer.

That evening, in an attempt to make things as non-threatening as possible for Ethan, we decide to attend 'Family Movie Night' at his new school. He was looking forward to it all week and I don't want to disappoint him. He has to be a little weirded out by my behavior earlier today in the car. However, as I attempt to sit through the movie and ingest popcorn, I realize I can't do either. *Why am I here?* It is all I can do not to break down in front of all of the families enjoying a night out together. I look around the dimly lit room and am so envious of the normalcy I assume everyone else is experiencing. How is it that they are able to carry on like that, focused on this inane movie about some stupid dog?

But wasn't that me, only yesterday? Twenty-four hours ago I'd have been chuckling right along with them. Now laughing seems foreign, a language I used to know, but can no longer speak. In fact, wasn't it merely last month that

I attended a breast cancer benefit and even made a donation on behalf of the 'victims'? Is that what I am now—a victim? I need to get out of here.

The next two days mush together into my worst weekend on record as I wander around in a stupor, barely eating. Brushing my teeth and showering now require internal pep talks and enormous effort. Surprisingly, I accomplish both Sunday morning before driving to the Family Day event for Grant's company at a park near the Rose Bowl. It is an uncharacteristically gray, chilly day for this time of year. Or is that just how I interpret my world now? I grab for a sweater on our way out the door.

There are all sorts of games and contests and food; I might even be having fun, if I was not convinced of my certain and imminent death. I attempt to distract myself by getting strapped into a harness hooked up to bungee cords that allow me to perform assisted back flips for Ethan. Clearly, he is unaware of my lack of actual skill and that it's the bungees doing the bulk of the work because he is clapping with an enthusiasm normally reserved for his dad. Even though I thoroughly enjoy impressing my son with my athleticism, after a few flips, I feel ill and request to be released.

There is a hired photographer wandering around, capturing moments for families and groups of friends.

"Let's get a picture today," I suggest to Grant. I don't mention that I want this day immortalized because it may be one of my last opportunities for a family photo before I fade away, and I want my husband and son to remember me.

Am I being dramatic or merely levelheaded and practical? I wish I knew.

"Sure," he says.

After the photo shoot, Grant offers me a bite of a cream puff he's been snacking on. Any other day I would accept it without hesitation, probably finish it off, and then be inclined to go get one of my own. But today the mere whiff of it makes me queasy. Fighting the unanticipated urge to throw up, I grimace and turn my head away. I didn't know that stress over being ill could make me feel so *ill*.

Grant, Ethan and me — mere days before my diagnosis

CHAPTER 3

"Crazy Train" – Ozzy Osbourne

Monday morning. The day of my surgical consultation has arrived. This is now the third morning I've been shaken awake by my new reality, its details rudely poking at me until I acknowledge their existence once again. Maybe I should sleep more. Of course, then I'd only wake up again to this assault. Somewhere, though, my brain still clings to the scrap of a possibility that at any moment I will be getting that liberating call, chock full of apologies and embarrassment about a misdiagnosis.

"We're so sorry, Mrs. Hosford," I can hear them saying, "we misread the slide with your tissue sample. Please, please forgive us!"

I won't even be mad. Actually, whoever calls will be shocked by my incredibly gracious attitude. "No worries," I'll say, with a casual wave of my hand, my voice sweet as the refined sugar I should have maybe tried harder to avoid. "Mistakes happen. Thank you so much for calling." No lawsuits threatened. No investigation. And no more cancer.

As I await the call and opportunity to display my forgiveness, a random thought occurs. Where is my period? I'm usually very regular. This stress is causing all sorts of issues with me—feeling ill yesterday at the picnic, delayed period, my boobs still sore. Is that part of breast cancer, for both breasts to ache?

"Steph, I think you should take a pregnancy test," Grant suggests when I list my current symptoms to him. Yeah, right.

I am in my bra and underwear, searching the closet for what to wear when we meet the surgeon in a couple of hours. I cup each hand over a boob and give a gentle squeeze. A little painful, but nothing dramatic.

"Honey, no," I respond, not looking away from my wardrobe. What does one wear to a meeting to discuss her breast's bleak future? Black? Depressing. Pink? It's way too soon to consider pink. "It's just a sign my period is still on the way, I'm sure of it." My reluctance is entirely justified. I have five years of secondary infertility to back it up.

"And I still think you should take one," Grant says in his typical, let's get answers so we can take action way. But this time he's really pushing it. Sure, there was a time in my life when a late period would have thrilled me with the possibility of pregnancy. But *now*, when there is cancer going on in there? I highly doubt my body is capable of such multitasking.

Besides the physical improbabilities, it makes no sense in my emotional world. For the past two years, the family portrait in my head consists of Grant, Ethan, our daughter who is yet to be named, and me. We are a smiling, happy bunch. I am holding my little girl in this portrait, her dark hair in pigtails.

On the second day of our marriage, Grant and I landed in Thailand for our honeymoon. During the incredibly long flight we had been chatting with a group of Americans who were all going to Southeast Asia to meet their babies for the first time and bring them home to the U.S. When the plane finally came to a stop at the terminal in Bangkok, Grant and I turned to each other in our cramped seats as everyone else scurried around us, popping open the overhead bins and trying not to brain each other with their luggage.

"I would like to do that one day." Grant said. "Adopt."

"Me too," I responded, grinning, grateful my new husband and I were on the same page. "For real, I'm not just saying it. I really want to."

Someday, regardless of how many biological children we had, we would fly back here to welcome a baby into our lives. I'd pictured the moment of my initial encounter with my daughter countless times, imagining her being placed in my arms. That moment was finally within sight.

Or it had been.

As much as I long to continue obsessing about when we will get word on the adoption and attempting to get a grip on the basics of Mandarin, my health crisis has taken center stage. Why would my body even think of messing with me further right now? It just doesn't make sense.

"I think it's ridiculous," I say to Grant, hands still on my boobs. "There is no way I'm pregnant, but if it will make you feel better, I'll do it."

I turn from the closet and take a few steps to the dresser. I pull open my underwear drawer and feel around. There it is—the test that was shoved to the back there months ago. It's not in a box. My hand closes around the sealed, smooth wrapper. I swore to myself I'd never use it, in an attempt to save my psyche from another negative result. I feel a folded rectangle of paper under it and grab that, too. It's an instruction sheet. Like I need one.

Why didn't I throw all this away, or donate it to Jenn? She has two beautiful children already and she's starting to think about trying for number three. This hopefully means, based on her past ease of productivity, she'll be in need of a test soon. At least it will probably be a positive readout for her.

I unwrap the test stick in the bathroom and hold it in my urine stream. I wait, washing my hands and face in the interim. I glance over at the test lying there on the vanity. Has it been four minutes? I pat my face dry with a towel and then return to the stick. I pick it up and take a step toward the trashcan. Wait, are those *two* pink lines beginning to appear?

My stomach tightens as I drop the stick back to the countertop and grab for the instructions rectangle. My fingers fumble with the eight hundred folds in the thin paper. Finally, I spread it out on the counter and scan the 'Reading the Results' section. Two lines = PREGNANT, of which I am already aware. But it can't hurt to double check, especially as I've obviously crossed an invisible threshold into an alternate universe. Did I wander too far into my closet a moment ago and come out the other side?

I look again to the stick. Still two pink lines, even darker now. What is happening? After all this time, my body chooses now to make two pink lines appear on that damn stick? I've waited so long to see those! My heart flutters with maternal instinct. But how can this be good? How the *hell* can this be good? No, this isn't happening. I don't believe it.

"Grant! We need to get another test. This one is wrong!"

CHAPTER 4

"Chasing Cars" — Snow Patrol

But it isn't wrong. And neither is the third positive test. I'm usually so organized, so prepared. Grant's dad even mentioned this competency in his speech at our wedding, although at the time I'd preferred he touch on my sense of humor or love of travel, or even my affinity for crossword puzzles, for God's sake. His words made me realize, though, that my need for a plan is not as covert as I'd thought. But *this*? I have no idea about this. Can there be a plan for handling this that isn't dreadful?

When I reveal my latest discovery to Mom, her reaction is similar to Grant's: guarded enthusiasm, apprehensive smile. I don't think any of us knows how to respond or what to feel right now. Perhaps we've entered a realm in which there are no pure emotions anymore, where all feelings are mixed, blended or pureed.

In the dreary exam room, Grant and I wait for the general surgeon. I have nothing to say right now. My mind draws blanks when I attempt to form any intelligible thoughts. My hand is on Grant's knee and I stare listlessly at the white wall.

"Good morning! I'm Dr. Conle. Congratulations!" says the tall pleasant-looking man in the blue surgical scrubs as he enters the room. What? His joyful exclamation has snapped me to attention.

"Did you read my chart? Do you know why I'm here?" I skip greetings and introductions. His light eyes darken a shade, cheeks slacken slightly as confusion sets in. And is that a hint of shame in his expression over not having taken the time to read more than the first fact printed in my chart before opening the door and his mouth?

He looks down at the paperwork in front of him and his original smile fades completely. "Oh, this pregnancy is *not* such a good thing. It's essentially feeding the tumor."

I wince at that t-word.

"The hormones associated with pregnancy are fueling the cancer to grow faster. You should terminate."

So that's it? I'm not allowed to incorporate the joy of that miraculous discovery into even one day? I begin to cry.

He leans forward. "Besides, your husband and son need you."

What is that supposed to mean? Does he think I've already made a decision to put the embryo's survival ahead of my own? I didn't know this is an 'it or me' situation. I don't know *anything* yet, for Christ's sake. So far this man has only added a layer of guilt to my plate that I am not ready to take on. I'm not ready for any of this. I could have lived my whole life knowing this would happen to me, and I still would never be ready for this. Ever.

I continue crying on and off throughout the appointment, during which Dr. Conle gives me a short physical exam and points out the despicable mass on my mammography film. I have to look away.

We briefly discuss the lumpectomy he will perform on my breast, assuming no other tumors are found. Other tumors? I'd never even considered that there could be more. Just the one is doing such a stellar job of ruining my life all on its own that I doubt it needs help.

Why is this happening to me? Why is my body being so

cruel? *I hate you. Here I take care of you all these years, exercising so much, eating right, going for my checkups. And now not only have you formed cancer behind my back, you also finally give me the pregnancy I've wanted for so long only to tease me? How could you?* It was hard enough to remove the lifeless embryo from my body a few years ago, but this one? This one is alive! And I need to give it up? It seems ridiculously unfair and all I want to do is go home to scream and cry. My lumpectomy is scheduled for October 12th, more than two weeks away.

Back home, I call to schedule the MRI for which Dr. Conle gave me a referral. "But I need to have the MRI NOW!" I plead with the scheduler. Can't she tell I'm losing my mind over this? Can't she cut me some slack?

"I'm sorry, Ma'am, but we are booked until October 8th."

"But I already know that this tumor is cancerous. And there could be more cancer in there," I feel ill and even slightly embarrassed revealing this about myself, like I'm admitting I'm damaged goods. At the same time, I'm irritated that I can't seem to get a little sympathy. "Shouldn't they fit me in first before other people? People *without* cancer?"

"Sorry, ma'am, but that's the soonest we can get you in." Shit.

The next day is spent either crying or conducting research on the internet, or both at the same time. I find out there are different types of breast cancer. The majority (85%) of breast cancer cells have hormone receptors for progesterone and/or estrogen, so it stands to reason that mine will turn out to be this type because I am pregnant and producing very high levels of these and other hormones. Finally, there is something I can understand! These cancers tend to be relatively slow growing and respond well to follow-up treatments like the drug Tamoxifen to keep them from recurring. Okay, I have that going for me. Oh, but heaven help the poor soul with the dreaded "triple negative" type of cancer, the type in which the cells do not contain hormone receptors and so can't be treated with follow up drugs. I grimace as I read about it. It tends to be aggressive, fast growing, and is clearly less desirable. Not that any of this is desirable, but already my standards are changing.

I am thinking along these lines the following day as I receive and open my 'Final Pathology Report' envelope regarding the samples taken during the core needle biopsy. This contains the details of the tumor, including the type of cancer it is. I pull out the report and scan the top page. TRIPLE NEGATIVE is written in bold in the first paragraph. No, no, no, no. Oh God. The air in the room dissipates instantly, just like a few days ago. I can't breathe. Desperately, I look for my name on the paper, hoping to see someone else's, wishing again for human error. But there it is—Stephanie Hosford. The walls are closing in and I could very well throw up.

This just can't be! I was just getting a grasp on maybe, possibly, why this is happening all at once—pregnancy, the hormones, then the cancer. Now I've been catapulted back into Hurricane What the Hell? "Grant!"

❖

That night I make the mistake of searching the internet again. 'Triple Negative' seems merely a euphemism for the

Grim Reaper as I read more about its "higher incidence of recurrence" and "lower survival rates."

Grant literally drags me away from the computer and turns it off. A potentially interesting fact I found, though, before being banished from the office, is that having the triple negative type of cancer could mean that the tiny embryo inside me is NOT feeding the tumor—they are separate, unrelated issues. What that might mean I am not yet sure. But for some reason, both my heart and brain agree that it possibly doesn't suck.

One thing is most definitely clear. I need medical attention and I need it now. I don't know exactly how unique my situation is, but I would guess very, especially if my family physician's reaction is any indication.

"*What?* But you were just in here last month, weren't you?" she asks me over the phone the next day.

Oh, I guess I forgot to wear my 'Alert! I Will Develop Breast Cancer and Become Pregnant Shortly. Please Be Prepared with Something Other Than Shock' t-shirt to that appointment.

"What do I do? Whom do I call?" I implore her.

"Um, um…let me think…I'm trying to think if I know anyone who has handled something like this," she says. *Please help me. Please come up with someone accommodating and extraordinary, or at least tell me how I can find someone like that.* "Well, it looks like Dr. Grable is the oncologist on your insurance plan, but he'll probably freak out at this, so let me talk to him first." Oh, no way. Not him.

Dr. Grable just happens to be the specialist who treated my dad a couple of years ago. My dad, who died of *cancer*. Not a 'strength' on the doc's resume in my opinion. I can't imagine being treated by someone I am so predisposed to dislike. Plus, apparently he is going to come apart at the thought of dealing with me.

"Okay," is all I can muster, as my palms start to sweat and my breath becomes shallow. Here I go again. I hang up and start crying. I am beyond lost.

"Honey, let me handle this part," Grant says later when I repeat the conversation with my doctor to him.

"I don't know what I'm doing, hon," I sniff, wishing I were not so overwhelmed by my situation. I've only made one call, and during it I could already feel myself getting flustered, emotions causing my words to get tangled up in my mouth. But Grant doesn't do that. I've never heard him get tongue-tied during an argument, a strength I find frustrating when I'm the on the opposing side of a marital squabble, but one I'm immensely grateful for now. I predict my case is going to require some salesmanship to doctors and our health insurance company. I'm not even sure what I'm trying to sell. I don't know what I'm supposed to be asking of them. "I'm so confused," I continue. "And I know our stupid insurance will fight us and make me see Dr. Grable."

"Screw them," he says. I manage a very slight smile.

I can only hope that if the tables were turned and Grant was the one with cancer I'd be able to pull it together and be helpful to him. I don't know that I'd be able to stay so calm when pleading such an important case. Luckily, I don't have enough space in my head to ponder this imaginary scenario any longer.

Three months ago, when I was healthy, or at least under that impression, I did not choose my primary care doctor based on the chance that I might someday need a first-rate oncologist. But that is how the HMO works. I can only see specialists within the same 'group' as my chosen primary physician, unless we want to pay for someone else all on our own.

I didn't think I could feel any worse about my situation, but now I see that I can. I begin to realize that not only have I single-handedly subverted our family plans, but I also might very well plunge us into bankruptcy.

Regardless, Grant is determined to get us appointments with champion specialists at reputable facilities. Both he and Mom ask friends for feedback, do online research and consult their own physicians for recommendations. Within a couple of days, the lists of names are combined onto an Excel spreadsheet containing each person's title, contact information, hospital affiliation, etc. Those who have been recommended at least twice are highlighted. I have been placed in charge of maintaining this spreadsheet due to my notable organizational skills. I'm glad to be able to contribute *something* to this endeavor other than just being the cause of it, although I can't help but get a knot in my stomach each time I make an entry. I close it immediately afterward, never leaving it open on the computer desktop. I name the spreadsheet simply "The List."

In addition to maintaining the spreadsheet on the computer, my job also includes keeping all of my physical records in a large file folder. The clearly labeled slots are filling up quickly with pathology reports, slides, mammography films, insurance info and a printed copy of 'The List.' I even have a slot labeled 'Research' which is meant for information gathered regarding pregnancy during cancer treatment. That slot is virtually empty, although I recently discovered that there was a woman who received chemotherapy while she was pregnant because she refused to abort for religious reasons. It seems like the baby was okay. It was a short article and there was no follow-up. Maybe it was fiction.

It has been one week since my positive pregnancy test but it feels like months.

"Okay, we have an appointment tomorrow morning," Grant announces, "and then another the day after tomorrow, and I have a call in to that oncologic gynecologist in Santa Monica."

"I've never even heard of an oncologic gynecologist. I can't imagine he's too busy," is my response because I'm too saddened to come up with anything more gracious. Can't I go back in time to five weeks ago and not have sex with Grant on whatever night that was? Things would certainly be easier now.

File folder in my hands, we set out in search of my future doctor. Our first stop: a well-respected institution whose location is technically West L.A., but there is also a convenient Pasadena branch. The oncologist here is a young gentleman who, contrary to what we thought, is not covered by our insurance.

"Oh, we accept that insurance, but only the PPO plan," the receptionist tells us as I present her my card. I told Grant earlier at some point that this might be a problem, but he was undeterred. Grant views such details as technicalities that he will work out later. Why, oh why, did we choose the HMO option during the last open enrollment? Oh yes, we decided that since we were sooooo healthy, maybe for once, we could save some money!

"Just this one time," I recall myself justifying, "and then next year, when we have *two* kids, and our little girl might have some special issues, we'll switch back to the PPO." *Someone* has 'special issues', that's for sure. And it's the same person who can hear her mother warning, "Never skimp on medical insurance because you never know…"

"We'll pay out of pocket," Grant informs the receptionist.

"Okay, that's $200 for the consultation. How would you like to pay for that?" Grant hands her his credit card. And so it begins. I want to cry as visions of our future home begin to fade, replaced by stacks of healthcare bills.

We are soon called in and led to an exam room. I change into the cotton robe and sit on the exam table. The doctor walks in shortly thereafter. Introductions are made and I receive a brief exam that consists mainly of his feeling around for the tumor. I realize how tired I am already of being felt up.

"Why don't you change back into your clothes and then come meet me in my office so we can talk."

"Alright," I say, stepping down from the table.

A few minutes later, Grant and I are sitting together, facing the doctor, a smooth mahogany desk separating us from him. Framed photos of his family are sitting on top of it, along with a computer and a few neat stacks of folders thick with paper. I glance around the office, appreciating the orderliness of it, but hating the blandness at the same time. Of course, what's he supposed to have? Suede covered beanbag chairs and lava lamps?

"So what should we do, Doctor?" Grant gets right to it.

"Well, following your surgery—you're getting a lumpec-tomy?" I nod. "Following surgery, I would recommend chemotherapy, six rounds, and then radiation." The room seems smaller all of a sudden, the doctor's voice so far away. I think he is still talking, but he sounds garbled.

"So you'd recommend chemo for sure, then?" I hear Grant ask. Good question. Maybe chemo is more of a suggestion in my case, something to consider but not super necessary.

"Oh, absolutely," is the immediate response. "Based on the aggressive nature of the cancer, I would definitely recommend chemotherapy." But the lump is so small. In fact, I think it felt smaller today in the shower, hardly even there.

"So then, what should we do about the pregnancy?" Grant asks.

"Oh, you would need to abort."

"And if it was your wife, would you tell her the same thing?" Yes, good move, Grant. Make it personal for him; change his perspective…and maybe his answer.

"I would absolutely tell her to abort and begin treatment right away," he answers, looking at me. His face softens a bit. I must look as defeated as I feel. He adds gently, "I'm sorry."

"Okay, thank you," is all I can whisper, essentially doubling the number of words I've uttered this entire visit. I guess we're done here.

The next day, we are on the freeway heading to another highly regarded institution. I know second opinions are important, but I don't want to go. I'd rather lie in bed. I'd rather be home, hugging Ethan and watching Power Rangers with him, wishing I could be a Power Ranger myself and back handspring my way out of this real-life mess. Ethan doesn't know much about my current crisis and I won't tell him more about it until I have a definite plan of attack. What's the point of informing him of a problem unless I can tell him how we plan to solve it?

My energy is already waning on this doctor quest, a good portion of it dissipated at yesterday's appointment, and now it's like a continuous slow leak deflating me with each passing moment. We park the car in the busy lot and head for the entrance. The buildings are tall and foreboding.

"It's cold in here," I tell Grant as we step inside through the sliding glass doors. He puts his arm around me. The large wooden door to Dr. Milbrook's office is heavy and a bit creaky as we enter the reception area. I check in as Grant finds a seat. I hand over my insurance card, which is again rejected, and then replace it with a credit card. I sigh and shake my head. I look at Grant and he gives a slight shrug.

This oncologist has been recommended by a friend of mine working in pharmaceutical sales. She hasn't actually met him, but a colleague of hers has a friend who was treated by him and says he's great. And apparently this patient of his is still in existence, so that's a positive start.

"Stephanie Hosford?" the nurse calls out into the room.

"Yes, right here." I stand up, grabbing my file folder. We follow her into the exam room where I change into another hospital gown, the same depersonalizing attire that I've been changing into far too much lately. My blood pressure and temperature are taken and then we wait. I'm not surprised my temperature is normal, but I was predicting my blood pressure would be somewhere off the charts because of all this stress, but no, it was normal, too, a little low even. Am I fading already?

Dr. Milbrook enters the room and introduces himself. He is short on small talk. He is older than Dr. Alford, his face more stern and his head more bald. He then begins and ends the exam. It's not that I want him feeling my breast for an extended time, but it seems he barely touched it, like we were merely passing each other in a narrow hallway and he accidently brushed it with his hand because he was holding someone's chart. Maybe he's so good that all he needs is to let his finger hover over patients for a moment to get a diagnosis.

"Let's go talk in my office."

So far I prefer Dr. Alford, not that I liked what he had to tell me yesterday. I change back into my clothes and Grant and I walk next door to Dr. Milbrook's office. He's sitting at his desk, which I'm fairly sure is a replica of Dr. Alford's desk, and now that I think about it, Dr. Hogan's, too. Apparently, they all use the same decorator.

He gestures for us to sit in the two chairs facing him. "So," Grant begins the conversation as we sit down, "what should be our plan, Doctor? We've been told Steph will need surgery and chemotherapy." Dr. Milbrook nods in agreement and looks down at my open chart.

"Yes, I would recommend six rounds of chemotherapy following surgery, based on age and cancer type." My stomach clenches as I hear those words again.

"And the pregnancy?" I ask this time, crossing my hands over my stomach.

"Well, I'd recommend abortion." I nod slightly and look toward the floor. "Actually, it's not unheard of that women have received cancer treatment while pregnant." I turn my head toward Grant, eyes wide. "But I wouldn't recommend it." My gaze shifts back downward.

"And if it was your wife? Would you say the same?" Grant tries this again.

"I'd tell her to abort so she could focus on herself."

I feel my soul deflate the rest of the way, like the inner tubes Jenn and I used to play with in the pool each summer.

By the end of the season, they were nothing but limp, mushy shells, useless and drained of fun.

When we get home, there is a message from the oncologic gynecologist. He can see us tomorrow. "Great," I tell Grant, not bothering to hide my sarcasm. "Set that right up. I'm sure it will be totally worth it. Money well spent." And then I go into our room to curl up and cry with no plans to emerge.

As we sit in traffic on the 405 Freeway creeping south the following morning, I have plenty of time to resent my current situation. I can't believe we are going to see a random doctor whose specialty is probably made up. I sigh and look over at Grant. "This is silly," I say, "going to see this doctor."

Grant continues looking straight ahead, taking a moment to respond. "Steph, I don't know. Maybe he'll have another perspective, some expertise to add because of his dual background. I'm doing my best here. I just want to cover all bases."

And then I want to cry again, but this time it's not because of what's happening in my body. It's because of the realization that I have been so dismissive of what Grant might be feeling about all of this. I actually haven't even reflected on it enough to be considered 'dismissive' because thoughts about Grant's feelings haven't entered my head at all. This is new territory for him, too. He doesn't want to be here on this freeway heading into the world of oncologic gynecology, but he is more than standing by me and so far I have been thankless. "I'm sorry," I say, holding back tears, "You're right. Maybe this guy can help us out."

Unfortunately, a few minutes into the appointment, I know this doctor is not going to be of assistance. After making it clear that the appointment is not covered by our insurance, so we will therefore owe him $300 today, he proceeds to suggest that I abort this baby, harvest some of my eggs and then freeze them. The eggs would be kept at this location — for a large monthly fee, of course. And then after all of my cancer treatment, he can surgically implant them in my womb. This is seriously his solution? How old will I even be when we attempt this? And with my less than fertile history, it sounds very…

"Sounds complicated," Grant tells him, reading my thoughts. And miserable and full of false hope and makes zero sense at all! Well, at least I didn't have to change into a hospital gown for this. It has been more of a meeting than an exam.

"Um, okay, I'll think about it," I tell him, wondering if he can detect my insincerity.

"Well, thanks for seeing us on such short notice," Grant tells him as he stands up and shakes the doctor's hand. Oh, good, we're done. I stand up, too, and we head toward the door.

"Oh, here. Take some information about in vitro fertilization," the doctor says, grabbing pamphlets and attempting to hand them to us.

"No thank you," Grant says, "but thanks for your time." I take the pamphlets, though, because I don't do well with rejection, even when it's not mine. The door closes heavily behind us and neither of us glances back at it.

So far, we've seen three specialists who have told me I should abort, and we've avoided the one on our insurance plan entirely to save *him* from having a stroke. Living in southern California, we could probably spend months going to consultations and gathering a mountain of opinions. Of course, this is assuming we could afford that, which we can't. And I suppose neither the cancer cells nor the embryonic cells would stop dividing while we continued the quest. And would any of those opinions be different anyway?

As uncomfortable as I am with what I've been told so far, it's looking like my path is inevitable. This baby's future is limited and I am sick with grief and guilt as we sit once again on the 405 Freeway, now inching north.

CHAPTER 5

"Killing In the Name" – Rage Against the Machine

Back home, I help Ethan into his costume of the day. He has chosen Spiderman and needs assistance with the Velcro closure on the back of it. Before I pull the edges together, I run my fingertips up and down his back, gently scratching his smooth skin with my nails. He giggles. "Yeah, back scratch, Mom," he says, taking a step backward toward me.

"Sure, babe," I reply, happy he took the bait before running off to play somewhere else. He's so hard to hold onto sometimes, always on the move, always chattering. But I can count on back scratches to keep him relatively quiet and with me while he enjoys his treatment. I want to pull him into my lap and hold him in my arms, rock him like when he was a baby. But I know he has villains to fight and webs to spin, so I give him a grand finale of scratches, a kiss on his soft, white little neck, and finish closing up the outfit.

"Now go have fun," I command.

"Thanks, Mom." He runs out of the room.

Ethan wants a sibling so badly. He's been requesting one for years, since he began noticing his friends gaining younger brothers and sisters. *We tried, Buddy.* And we came so close, but then… I bury my face in my hands, wondering how and if I could ever explain all of this to him.

"I'm sorry. I'm sorry, little baby," I whisper to my stomach. "And I'm sorry, little baby," I speak out loud, toward China. I burst into tears as the likelihood of losing two children sinks in. I never really had these children to begin with, but it doesn't matter. I will never hold either of them. One will never get a chance in this world at all and the other will go to another family or maybe live her life in an orphanage, never understanding how she was meant to be with me, to be *my* daughter, but now I've let them both down. I've let everyone down.

It is Grant who finds me on Ethan's tic-tac-toe rug, soggy and defeated. "Let's just go back to that first guy and get it over with," I mumble. "Which one?" he asks, sitting down next to me, but first lifting me upright so I can lean on him.

"The guy with the desk," I say, knowing that doesn't help. I'm so tired. "The one in Pasadena," I manage, barely audible. I reach for a Kleenex.

"Oh. Well, I have one more appointment for us," Grant says. I pull back from him and look at his face. He's serious.

"No!" I shake my head. "I'm not doing this again. I can't." What is he doing? He is so much more practical than this. Don't tell me he's losing it, too, because then I will know we are truly doomed.

Grant is generally very even-keeled and I love this about him. He makes decisions based on the facts presented. In other words, on any given day he's more emotionally grounded than I am. I'm nervous because it seems like maybe he's losing some of the stability I've been relying on for the past decade. On the other hand, Grant is also one of the most competitive people I know, which is good for business and sports, but I hope he is seeing the whole picture here and not being ruled by his stubborn streak. I think we both know the distressing tasks that lie ahead. Does he really think another doctor will tell us anything different?

"Listen, I know it's hard," he says, "but there's one more place that has gotten several recommendations. I think it's worth checking out. If they tell us the same thing, then we'll know for sure." I still don't want to go, but I can tell Grant needs this appointment before throwing in the towel.

"Where is it?" I ask.

"City of Hope." I pull back again. Oh, no.

Although I've never been there, I'm familiar with City of Hope. It's a well-known and respected cancer institute that is actually closer to our house than any of the other places. However, I am more than slightly repulsed because I know they treat very sick people and there is no way I could possibly be associated with *that* sorry lot...right? Oh, God.

But Grant has been working so hard to get me these appointments quickly, not allowing schedulers to delay us and convincing them of the urgency of my problems. I can't believe that I am considering agreeing to this cancer consultation as a gift to Grant, but this is where we are. I used to give much better gifts.

"Okay, let's go. But this is it, please."

"You're right. I think we'll have enough to go on after this one. They need your slides, though, so their lab can test the tissue samples."

"Alright," I concede, although I'm annoyed with the added task of again calling Medical Records for this appointment I find so unnecessary. They should be on my speed dial by now.

I am struck by a blast of hot air upon exiting the car in the city of Duarte the next morning. These Santa Ana winds bring to mind what it might be like to be trapped inside a hair dryer. I can't say it is lightening my mood. Grant and I walk through the parking lot, my hair whipping me in the face, leaves skittering around the asphalt.

Despite the winds, City of Hope definitely has a much more welcoming atmosphere than the other places. I look around us as we make our way to the entrance. There is a large circular reflecting pool out front with a fountain at its center topped by a bronze statue of a man and a woman holding a baby high in the air. It's beautiful. People are sitting on the benches surrounding the pool, either reading alone or chatting quietly with someone else. We pass them as we enter the main building. I glance back at that bronze baby once more and feel a twinge of longing.

We check in, hand over my slides, and are then escorted by a volunteer over to the Women's Center. It smells nice as we walk along an outside path between buildings. I glance around and realize this is due to the rose bushes on either side of us. This place is reminding me how little time I've taken to seek out any type of tranquility. I've taken no time, really, having been far too busy melting down instead.

I haven't even listened to my iPod lately, which is my customary source of therapy. In light of my new reality I think I'll be purchasing more songs soon, expanding my playlists exponentially.

We are called into an exam room. After changing into yet another shapeless gown, I sit on one of the molded plastic chairs and wait. I have not yet committed to the exam table. Footsteps pause outside my door and then I hear the familiar metallic sounds of a door handle being operated. In walks Dr. Santos holding my chart, which he places on the counter. "Good morning," he says with a smile, "I am Dr. Santos, one of the oncologic surgeons here." I like his accent. He is a pleasant-looking man, a little less than average height, probably in his late 50's, with wavy salt and pepper hair. His face conveys a certain serene wisdom, like that of an enlightened guru. He has a warm handshake for Grant, the type where he holds Grant's hand in both of his, and then he walks over to me and gives me a hug—a *hug*?

"Well, Stephanie, I've read your story," he says as he releases me and walks over to retrieve the chart. I am still in shock from the hug. "I see that you have triple negative breast cancer, which our lab has confirmed from the slides we got from Dr. Wilson." They've confirmed this already? That is a sad, albeit impressively quick, verification. I don't really expect anything different, although maybe I've clung to a shred of belief in a misdiagnosis. That shred has now officially disintegrated, no, *vanished*, because 'disintegrated' might leave some molecules of hope behind and I can't afford to have them floating around in my head.

"Yes," is all I say.

"Would you mind sitting on the table so I can perform a short exam?" he asks, motioning toward it. Where is his accent from? Italy? South America? Russia? Probably not a large Santos contingent in Russia. I love accents, but I'm not great at pinpointing their origins. It's the main reason I am not an international spy. That, and I'm really bad at driving backward.

"Okay," I agree and climb up. "Where is your accent from?" He feels for the tumor, then carefully palpates around in my armpit, and then moves on to the right side for a bit. "Spain," he answers, fingers pressing gently but firmly around my collarbone. I watch his face for a change in expression and brace for a concerned "hmmmm," but neither of those happens.

"Well, I only feel the one tumor on the left and it seems

to be a little over a centimeter, which is not big, but we'd have to get you an MRI to be sure," he tells me. I like his use of 'we' for some reason.

"Oh, I have one scheduled already in about a week," I tell him, "and then a lumpectomy to follow. But neither one of those is being done here at City of Hope."

"Alright," he says, and then proceeds to place a piece of plain white paper over my chart and grab a pen from his lab coat pocket. Okay, I suppose he is done with me. I expect he is about to write 'CASE CLOSED', or something to that effect, on the paper and place it in the front of my chart. "Let me explain how the lumpectomy will work." No one's done this for me yet, not even Dr. Conle, who will be performing the operation.

"But I'm not getting it done here," I repeat.

"Yes, I know," he smiles, not heading for the door. "I just want to explain the procedure for you and some alternatives." Dr. Santos then sketches a profile of a breast and maps out the lumpectomy, step by step, including how my lymph nodes will be tested for any spread of cancer. He tells me I could opt for a mastectomy, too, if I want to be more aggressive. The simple mention of the m-word makes me break into a cold sweat though, so I'll stick with the original plan.

"And what about after the surgery? Will I need chemotherapy?" I ask him after I feel I have a grasp on my surgical future.

"Yes, chemotherapy is the next step due to the aggressive nature of the triple negative cancer." Shoot. Time to give up on that dream, too, I suppose.

"You know," he continues, "have you thought about genetic counseling?" I haven't. So far, the only counseling I've assumed I will need is psychiatric.

"I'm the only person I know in my family to have ever had breast cancer, so no," I answer.

"Do you have any Ashkenazi Jewish heritage?" he asks. Interesting question. Is my condition somehow related to my kinship with the 'Chosen People'? If so, it's yet another awesome thing to be chosen for.

I think of my parents, east coast Jews, one Czechoslovakian and German, the other Russian and Polish, obviously eastern European, which translates to 100% Ashkenazi. Dad's Jewish pride was always bubbling close to the surface, despite his unapologetic atheism. I remember the eye rolling when I came home from elementary school one day singing the "Johnny Appleseed" song because it "thanked the Lord." And just hearing the word 'Mercedes' could launch a tirade against all of "those Nazi bastards." But when I asked him why he purchased a shiny new red Mustang considering Henry Ford was such a notorious anti-Semite, he grinned and said he was actually giving Ford the middle finger by doing that. "He'd turn over in his grave, the bastard," Dad said, "if he knew Norm Abrams was driving his car!"

Of course, then there's Mom, Jewish Lite, boycotting most German products, but who mainly calls upon her Judaism when threatened by other religions, for example at my wedding when she made sure Grant's gentile foot smashed the wine glass at the conclusion of the ceremony. It was more of a statement than a belief.

Whatever the Jewish connection is to my present situation, if it can lead me to answers as to why I got cancer, I'm willing to listen. And so I respond, "I do, actually. Why?"

Dr. Santos explains that there is a genetic mutation called BRCA 1 or 2, and that people with an Ashkenazi

Jewish background tend to carry it more often than those of non-Jewish backgrounds. Oy vey.

"So it's like Tay-Sachs, right? Or sickle-cell anemia? People of similar background stick together and eventually it can lead to problems that get continually passed down to offspring."

"Pretty much," Dr. Santos says.

I'm glad Grant and I mixed things up a bit with our marriage, genetically speaking. Dr. Santos then goes on to explain that the mutation can increase the chances of developing breast cancer by up to 80%, and ovarian cancer by 40%. I should consider being tested for these genetic factors at some point, he suggests, because if I test positive, it might have an impact on preventative measures I take to avoid a second occurrence. I can't begin to process the thought of another cancer occurrence, as I am barely able to wrap my head around the first one. However, I do appreciate the time Dr. Santos takes to educate us.

"I'll think about that," I tell him, caught between wanting answers and not wanting to be tested further or add another appointment to my agenda.

"Thank you, doctor," I say and hop off the table, reaching for my clothes folded neatly on a chair. Despite Dr. Santos's humanity, I, for one, am done for the day. I believe I have a hold on what needs to happen and I am feeling the urge to go home for my daily wallowing session, followed by a round of not eating. As I take my tank top from the pile, I realize we haven't discussed the pregnancy. I guess I should mention it, although I so don't want to hear those words again. I turn around to face Dr. Santos.

"So when would be the best time to abort?" There. I said it first. *I* own it, not him. "Can it be done when I get the lumpectomy?" Might as well strive for efficiency. Dr. Conle and Dr. Hogan work at the same hospital, after all. I look over at Grant and he has already closed his notebook, the pen clasped to the top of it.

Dr. Santos places my chart on the exam table and says slowly, "I'm sure that could be arranged, if that's what you want...but you know, it's not necessary to abort. We can treat you while you're pregnant."

I cross my arms in front of me and stare at him in silence, waiting for him to smirk, point a finger at me and say, "Gotcha! We'd never do that. Now go get an abortion." Or he's at least about to give an exasperated sigh and shake his head at the thought of dealing with me. I wait, but when neither of those happens, I realize I should probably respond in some way. However, as this is usually the part where Grant and I are clearing out and heading for the parking lot, I am at somewhat of a loss. I make an attempt to reply to Dr. Santos.

"B-but the other doctors...they all said they are all telling me it's better to terminate the pregnancy..."

Grant stands up and cuts in. "But what about Stephanie? Isn't it better for her if we abort?" I notice our notebook has been reopened on the table.

"Not necessarily," Dr. Santos says. "Abortion of the baby would not improve the mother's chances of surviving breast cancer."

Did he say 'mother'? For the first time, an image of me holding a newborn flashes through my mind. I want to reach out and grasp it, put it in my pocket to keep, but it darts away too quickly. Grant counters, "But we were told that the pregnancy hormones are fueling the cancer."

"That might be true in other cases," answers Dr. Santos.

"Because Stephanie is triple negative—do you know what that is?" We nod. "The cancer is not responsive to those hormones."

"And the baby?" I ask, yearning for the image to return. "How risky is it *really* for the baby if I go through chemo?"

"Well," he continues, "from what we've seen, the percentages of abnormalities that occur in the babies are in line with the general population, so it is believed that the chemotherapy drugs you would receive won't affect the fetus."

"And you would do this? You would do this for me?" I ask, still clutching my tank top, not wanting to let go of *anything* right now.

"Yes," he says, "we would."

Grant and I are silent for most of the way home. I look out at the blue sky, the puffy white clouds like cotton balls that have been pulled and stretched by playful fingers. Just before our freeway exit, I notice my cheeks are a bit achy. I reach up to feel them and realize I'm smiling. I haven't used these muscles in so long, I suppose, that they are now easily fatigued. Grant reaches for my hand. I look over at him and I predict his cheeks are going to be tired today, too.

That evening, after dinner, I take my first prenatal vitamin.

CHAPTER 6

"Lay Me Down" – The Dirty Heads

My MRI is a week away. There is really nothing for me to do except curl up in the fetal position on the bed in the dark and feel sorry for myself. My initial spark of hope from the consultation with Dr. Santos lasted only a few hours and has now been essentially extinguished by feelings of dread for what lies ahead. Is this venture at all realistic? Even if it is technically possible, it's remarkably daunting. And I don't even have an oncologist yet. I know Dr. Santos said they'd treat me over at City of Hope, but he's a surgeon. Is there really an oncologist there who would be as kind and positive and amenable as he was? I also haven't checked if our insurance covers City of Hope. Rather than search for any answers, I have chosen to hole up in the bedroom and feel guilty and disgusted with myself for thinking that it was almost easier when doctors were telling me to abort. Now I have a choice to make. All of this lies with me. Can I handle going through with either option?

I am shaken from my cocoon of self-torment by an acquaintance of Mom's, a breast cancer survivor, who stops over with a gift. I'm grateful it's not a flower arrangement, blooming with pity and condolences. Inside the box she hands me is what can only be described as a 'cancer kit'. This might be harder to take than flowers. I smile feebly as she explains the usefulness of each item.

"...And these ski caps will come in handy later, especially at night because your head will get cold," she says, grinning, obviously pleased with her spirit of giving. There are self-help books, body lotions I've never heard of, and a whole lot of pink in that box, too. These tokens are not helping me. I'm not ready.

"Right…" I respond quietly, trying to mask my bitterness and hold back my tears.

On some level I realize this woman is only trying to help, attempting to bond with me in what will become our shared experience, but what I really want to do is throw it back in her face and tell her to get the hell out of here. I don't want this glimpse into my frightening future, a future when I will need things like ski caps for my cold, exposed head and skincare products 'designed especially for those going through cancer treatment.' When she finally leaves, I retreat back to my dark cell of a room to curl up once again.

An hour later, I have another visitor. My cousin Pam knocks gently on the door, enters and sits down on the foot of the bed. "How ya doin', sweetie?" she asks, stroking my arm. I've always enjoyed spending time with Pam. She's a consistently fun, smiling, big-sister-I-never-had type of girlfriend, always up for a glass of wine, a quality chat and a lot of laughs. I rejoiced the day she officially became part of our family by marrying my cousin Bill. I turn over to look at her. She is not smiling now.

In fact, her green eyes, so striking against her dark red hair, are filled with tears. I sit up and start crying, too, and we hug. It actually feels good to cry with someone else, even if we are both crying for me. I am grateful that Pam didn't begin with a pep talk about the power of positive thinking. Mom has been doing this a lot lately, telling me to "Stay positive" and "Think only positive thoughts" and I have been finding that truly impossible. I am scared, I am mad and I am dealing with a certain amount of self-pity, which is partly why I'm mad, because I've never respected self-pity. But right now, I long to express my negativity aloud and have it viewed as acceptable.

"I can't believe this is happening to me," I sob, "I just don't know why this is all happening at once. And I don't want to die yet. I don't want to die." Yes, I said it. I said "die" and I know Pam can take it. I don't have to feel guilty about scaring her like I do with Mom or even Jenn.

"I know, honey, I know," Pam says, still hugging me. After another minute, she pulls back slightly and looks me in the eyes.

"You're going to get through it, you know," she says, her face more serious than I've ever seen it. I look down and keep silent.

"Hey," she lifts up my chin, "you're going to get through it...and so is that baby...and you're going to have your baby girl from China, too. You're going to do it all." I know Pam wouldn't bullshit me. She's not the type to bullshit anyone. If she didn't think I could do this, she wouldn't encourage it. But this is the first time someone has mentioned the adoption in conjunction with everything else. I've been pushing it to the side for a couple of weeks, scared to think too much about it, knowing that at some point it will need to be addressed...but *could* I actually do it all?

"Oh, why is this happening all at once?" I moan again, flopping back down onto the pillow. "There is so much decision making to be done and the clock is ticking away so quickly. I don't have time to process this properly."

"Well, sometimes maybe it's better not to have all the time in the world to overanalyze," Pam says, knowing how

I usually roll. "Sometimes you just have to jump in and go for it."

The phone rings and I hear Mom answer it somewhere outside my room. I hear her walking down the hallway toward my closed door, chatting on the phone. I hope it's not for me. Knock, knock, knock. Shoot. "Steph? Grant's on the phone." I am relieved it's Grant. He's probably checking in, telling me he'll pick up Ethan from the extended program at school on his way home. "Okay, thanks, got it," I tell Mom as I pick up the receiver next to the bed. I look at Pam as I answer.

"Hi Honey."

"Hi, how are you feeling?"

"Okay, I guess. Pam's here."

"Good," he says, "we're leaving for Maui tomorrow."

"Right. Wait, what? Maui?"

Pam's eyes widen and so does her smile. She is nodding her head yes, clearly in utter approval of this spontaneous travel arrangement. "See?" she says after I've hung up, "sometimes you just have to go for it. No time to think. Just go."

I tilt my head and imagine lush tropical gardens, cascading waterfalls and swaying coconut palms on beaches of fine white sand. I guess if I'm going to be depressed and perplexed, it's more enjoyable to be that way in Maui.

The next day we step off an airplane into plumeria-scented paradise. I'm afraid to ask how much this is costing us. The reason we are going on this trip is terrible, but it quickly proves a welcome escape from all the doctors, tests, test results, and of course my darkened room.

It's a shame my current physical, mental and emotional state will preclude me from partaking in sex or alcohol as a trip like this would normally call for plenty of each. Maybe next time. Please let there be a next time.

I spend hours reading and watching Grant and Ethan paddle out into the Pacific on their longboards with the many other pale-legged tourists, practicing what they just learned during their surf lesson while I sip virgin piña coladas, my feet comfortably buried in the warm fine sand. We go kayaking, enjoy a luau, drive partway to Hana (turning the car around due to Ethan's constant complaints about how "boring" it is — I guess at 6 years old, if you've seen one gorgeous, breathtaking waterfall, you've seen them all), and get in a fair amount of quality snorkeling.

I love to snorkel. I've always enjoyed the serenity, the feeling that I am flying gracefully over bustling underwater cities, observing the sea life as it goes about its business. I also appreciate that should an equipment malfunction arise (e.g. water in the snorkel or mask) it can be fixed quickly and easily so that I can safely resume snorkeling. Grant, on the other hand, prefers SCUBA diving. He is never annoyed by the heavy oxygen tank or weight belt strapped to him, nor does he have qualms about being completely at the mercy of this equipment or a hopefully quick thinking 'buddy' should the provisions fail. Although I know he would rather be off chasing sea turtles or far beneath the water exploring a shipwreck, Grant has agreed to another morning of snorkeling with me.

As he and Ethan venture off on their own for a while, I am left floating face down on a bright green blowup raft, peering through a cutout hole at the brilliantly colored fish and coral.

Abruptly, I am overcome with queasiness. I assume it's the motion sickness I've become increasingly sensitive to with each passing year, but as I lift my head up and look around, hair and mask dripping salt water, I see the ocean is exceedingly calm. In the distance I see some other members of this excursion to Molokini kicking around rather spastically, but they are too far to have any significant effect on my raft. I work hard to control myself, mortified by the thought of leaving a mass of vomit in this tranquil, turquoise section of the world. I paddle back to the tour boat, climb aboard and turn in my flotation device. I'm the first one back, and I assure the 'captain' that I am having a great time. "I'm just tired," I tell him, hoping I'm not the same color as the sea kelp.

I sit on a smooth wooden bench, focus on the horizon and hope for the best. If I recall, when pregnant with Ethan, I dealt with a low-grade, unpleasant feeling of constant nausea for the first twelve weeks. Curiously, broccoli had the power to intensify this feeling. The mere thought of it could make my palms sweat. Is all that starting again? As a test, I envision some broccoli, its large flower head and leafy stalk, and the evidence is irrefutable—I do indeed feel more ill. I take several slow deep breaths, trying as hard as I can not to whimper on the exhale.

It is true, I accept over the next couple of days as my woozy condition persists. Morning sickness has arrived, and there is not much I can do about it. The ginger snaps I found at the tiny market near our hotel provide only minimal relief. But despite the additional discomfort nausea adds to my life, I don't entirely hate it. It provides a certain amount of security as it lets me know the tiny being who is sharing my body is still hanging in there. I have not yet committed fully to a plan, but deep down in that part of one's soul where everything is true, where fear and frustration and guilt have been stripped away, I want this baby. I am happy knowing it's there. But can I really do all this? And would I be doing the right thing by trying? How I long to go back to grappling with my normal daily decisions such as what jeans I should wear or if I should make pizza or order one.

On our fourth and final night as we lay in bed, Ethan asleep between us rather than on his own bed. I gather up the courage to feel that damn little cancer nugget in my breast. I've been avoiding touching that area because it makes me so angry and terrified to know it is still there. I impotently wish it has miraculously dissolved on its own, but there it is, hard and unyielding under my fingertips. "Just get OUT!" I yell at it and then start crying. "Out, out, out!" Grant turns to me and reaches over Ethan to lay his hand on my shoulder. "They're going to get it, hon. You're going to be okay. We will *all* be okay." I nod my head and try unsuccessfully to fight the tears. I've cried more these past two weeks than ever in my life. I don't know how my overworked lacrimal glands have not gone on strike and halted tear production altogether.

As we board the plane back to L.A., I am filled with trepidation about the reality to which I am returning. I also have a nervous energy running rampant throughout my system that is not unlike what I have felt before the few triathlons that I have participated in. Sure, I'm probably about to get my ass kicked, but can we just get started already? I just want to finish. I'm not after a trophy.

The day after our return, Grant accompanies me to my MRI appointment. Upon arriving, I learn that I will be intravenously given a contrast dye called gadolinium, which is supposed to increase the visibility of my breast tissue. I follow the technician down the hallway to a small changing room. She opens the curtain and motions for me to step in. "I'm six weeks pregnant, by the way," I say casually, stepping past her. She has her hand on the curtain to close it but instead quickly lets go.

"We can't give this to you then," she tells me shaking her head. "It's not safe for the baby."

"Then I won't get the IV."

"You have to," she insists. "It's the only way to get accurate results." Did she just punch me in the stomach?

"What am I supposed to do then?" I implore her as I sink down onto the metal chair that takes up half the space in the changing room. I put my face in my hands. I wait for any answer, but nothing comes out of her mouth. I look up at her.

"Um...," she says and offers a slight shrug.

Suddenly, I throw my hands up and declare, "Fine, then I'll abort." I glare at her, daring her to counter.

It isn't entirely fair to put this random woman on the spot like this, but I have had it with this roller coaster. I can't believe I was so hopeful just yesterday. What an idiot I was to think I could actually keep this baby! Jesus. I'm already having unforeseen obstacles thrown at me and I am clearly not suited to deal with them. This can only be viewed as a harbinger of things to come if I go through with the pregnancy. I will always be wondering if I am causing permanent damage to the fetus, or whether I'm placing myself at risk by not having a certain procedure.

I begin to cry as I once again stumble into the quicksand of self-doubt. Rather than throwing me a rope or a branch or even a twig, the tech merely watches me flail and sink, my chart still in her hand. Grant must have heard my unexpected and rapid meltdown from the waiting area because he steps into the room. He is briefed by the tech on what has just transpired here, tells both of us that this is way too big of a decision to make at this moment without all the facts, and then leads me outside. "Put us down for tomorrow at this time," he tells them on our way out.

We spend the next hour in the hospital atrium calling Dr. Wilson and other radiologists for their opinion on the safety of this procedure during pregnancy. Grant is actually the one doing this while I pace nervously around him in circles. The consensus is that there *is* no true consensus because no research has been officially done on this matter. Lack of prior human experiments aside, the doctors do all seem to agree that the MRI itself shouldn't cause a problem. If anything, it would be the contrast dye, but the gadolinium is indeed necessary. Should the embryo be affected, it will simply terminate on its own. If it's not, it should be fine. Or in my case, I suppose, waiting for the next round of toxins to fend off. Was I seriously in Maui just yesterday snacking on macadamia nuts?

I sigh. "Well, tiny thing," I tell it, looking at my abdomen, "I guess this is the first test you need to pass."

The following morning I proceed with the MRI, drink about a gallon of water in an attempt to flush the dye from my system, and wait.

A couple of miscarriage-free days later, the results of

the MRI show that there is only the one tumor on the left side, it looks to be under 2cm, and there is nothing unusual detected in the other breast. In summary, Baby is still clinging to my uterine wall for dear life and the tumor is working alone. I consider it a good week.

But I have one more appointment to go. My surgery is scheduled for Monday and I need to meet with Dr. Conle this afternoon to go over the details of it. Grant leaves work early and picks me up. Morning sickness has tightened its grip on me, making the twenty-minute car ride to Dr. Conle's office seem like two hours. Of course, my agitation exists on both physical and emotional levels so it is difficult to isolate any one cause and know its true contribution to my overall discomfort. Regardless, it all adds up to the constant feeling that I'm about to address a huge crowd of people and give a speech on something I know nothing about.

"How are you?" asks Dr. Conle. This is such a loaded question these days. I'm somewhere between sick and well, I suppose, existing in some sort of nebulous atmosphere that I haven't yet gotten a grip on.

"Ok, considering," I answer. "We went to Maui," I add, looking over at Grant, "thanks to my husband."

"Oh, nice. You have a great husband."

Yes, I do. And I'd so much rather be holding hands with him on the beach, watching Ethan dart in and out of the warm, foamy tide as it ebbs and flows. But instead, I'm sitting here on a chair covered in scratchy fabric in a chilly office, about to discuss the carving of my body.

Reluctantly, I turn back to Dr. Conle. "It looks like we can get away with a partial mastectomy," he says.

"What? What is that?" I ask nervously, "I thought I was getting a lumpectomy."

"Oh, you are, it's the same thing, just sometimes called a partial mastectomy."

Well, I don't like it. I'm picturing a weird half-boob now, whereas with a lumpectomy I imagined a whole boob with a new scar. Which will it be?

"What will that look like afterward?" I ask, having visions of a small, misshapen breast.

"The tumor appears small, so it shouldn't be too disfiguring."

Not *too* disfiguring?

"The surgery should take about three hours, during which I will remove the tumor and some surrounding tissue to get a clear margin. So what I remove is always slightly bigger than the tumor itself."

"But it looks small, right, the tumor?" I am quick to ask.

"It appears small, but we won't know exactly until I go in there. These tumors can be tricky, spreading out sneakily in various directions," he says as he points his long index finger up, then down and then left and right. I picture him tunneling around in my boob, scooping out cancer the way I follow the trails of chocolate chips in cartons of mint chip ice cream, sometimes needing to go deep. It's never pretty in there when I'm done.

"Before I remove the tumor," Dr. Conle explains, "I will be injecting it with a radioactive dye and following the dye with a special instrument to see if any cancer has spread to the lymph nodes." Wait, did he say radioactive? That can't be good for a developing fetus.

"Did you say radioactive?"

"Yes."

"Is that considered safe for the baby?"

"No, it's not," he affirms, raising his eyebrows. He's clearly confused. Ah, poor guy, so much has happened since the consultation two weeks ago. I can't blame him for assuming I am going to abort, as that is essentially how we ended our last meeting.

"And you will need to sign a contract stating that you are terminating the pregnancy so that I can perform that part of the procedure." Oh, is he about to be surprised.

"Um, I'm trying to keep it for now, actually," I reveal, "the baby."

"Really?" he looks at me like I've just told him I recently had lunch with a leprechaun.

"Yes," Grant answers, not intimidated by Dr. Conle's expression or tone. "We've met with City of Hope and they said they'd treat Steph while she's pregnant, so we're going to try." I sit up a little straighter.

"And I've read that fetuses are fine when the mom is under general anesthesia. Is that true?" I ask.

"Usually, yes," he agrees after a pause, "but if you're going to do this, then instead of the dye injection, we will have to surgically remove a cluster of lymph nodes and dissect them to check for cancer. Not a huge deal. I've done it many, many times—but there will be more scarring and maybe some other problems later, like lymphedema."

"I've heard of that. What would that be like?"

"Your arm swells up like a balloon and you wear a compression sleeve to try to control it. It's not fun to deal with."

"But isn't that just a temporary issue right after surgery if it happens at all?"

"Actually, it could happen at any time…the risk would be

there for the rest of your life." Okay, so I am clearly not the expert I thought I was.

"Plus," he continues, "there will be a loss of sensation on the back section of your arm that may or may not come back." Oh.

"It's also a longer and more difficult recovery because you will have a drain coming out of your armpit for a couple of weeks collecting fluid." That sounds...gross.

"Okay," I respond, trying to avoid focusing too much on that armpit thing.

"Alright then, I'll see you Monday morning." We all stand up. "And before you leave today, though, you'll need to sign some paperwork. It states I've told you everything I just said, but that you still refuse to abort." I nod my head.

What am I doing? I wonder for the thousandth time as we are leaving Dr. Conle's office. I just placed my signature on papers saying I 'refuse to abort', despite the warnings. I don't know whether to feel like a hero or an idiot. But I do feel that I should give this little life force a chance. Hell, if it can survive the MRI *and* surgery on its own, then it's one badass little fetus and badass fetuses deserve badass mommies. Maybe there's one around here somewhere?

Grant is unlocking the car for us to get in when I realize something. What if this fetus I am attempting to keep isn't even there anymore? When I had my miscarriage two years ago, I was clueless to the fact that there was no heartbeat until I went in for my regularly scheduled appointment. What if this one's heart has stopped, too, and I am equally clueless this time? I look over at Grant. "We need to go to Dr. Hogan's, *now.*"

I call Dr. Hogan on our way there and inform the receptionist I'll be in his office in ten minutes for an ultrasound. Hmm, it feels kind of good to command rather than ask for something. Is this what it's like to be badass? "Um, o-okay," she says when I tell her of my imminent arrival.

Seven minutes later, I march on in to the office, head straight through the waiting area and into a vacant exam room, strip off my underwear from under my skirt and assume the position in the stirrups.

"Let me know if it's worth it," I instruct Dr. Hogan when he enters. "Please," I add. He gives me a quizzical look, but does proceed with my demands.

"Well," he says, as he moves the lubricated transducer probe around inside my uterus, "the heartbeat is quite strong for being just six weeks along."

"That's a good sign, right?" I ask him, looking for some encouragement. "I'm doing the right thing by keeping it, right?"

He doesn't answer, or even look me in the eye for that matter. He puts the machine back in order and then scribbles something in my chart.

"We'll monitor you," he says finally, toward the nurse.

CHAPTER 7

"The Sweet Escape" – Gwen Stefani

Monday morning. It's been only two weeks since my diagnosis and pregnancy discovery, which seems utterly impossible. How can it be that three weeks ago I attended the 'Howdy Coffee' at Ethan's new school? That morning, paper cup in hand, I wandered around the school's courtyard, meeting and greeting other parents, speaking to the seasoned PTA moms about annual fundraisers and the seemingly endless ways I could volunteer my time. I eagerly signed up for eight committees, looking forward to being involved and useful.

A week later, I withdrew from all of it, assuming I couldn't handle these new commitments in any competent, sane way.

"I'm sorry," I told the Parent Volunteer Coordinator. "An issue has come up. It's personal."

"Is everything okay?" she asked.

"I...I don't know," I answered cryptically before hanging up. Who knows what she thinks is going on with me, other than I am a total flake, but I'm sure whatever it is she's imagining can't be any worse or more bizarre than the reality. Thankfully, at Mountain Avenue Elementary there is a car line option for both drop off and pick up of students, so I can carry on with the anti-social behavior I instituted after my diagnosis.

Before that, I might have been described as sociable, friendly, someone who smiles a lot. Now, I'm probably viewed as a standoffish hermit, if anyone notices me at all. I realize I'm choosing to cloister myself at home, but after all these doctor visits, both scheduled and the occasional drop-in, driving all over town, MRI's, and impromptu jaunts to Maui, I am too worn out for small talk. What would I say to these parents? I'd like to explain that I hope my usual amicable demeanor is only temporarily deferred rather than forever unavailable, but there is no way I'm going to. I don't even know anyone yet. It's easier to fly under the radar.

We go to the hospital to check in. Mine is a 'day surgery', so I'll be going home this afternoon, if all goes as planned—which it should, but I need to sign about a dozen forms stating that I realize anything could happen, including death—mine, that is. I am surprisingly calm as I change into my hospital gown, despite a certain amount of anxiety about being stuck with an IV needle. I just want to get on with this and get this friggin' little cancer ball out of my boob and my life.

From my hospital bed in the pre-op area, I tell absolutely anyone who works here and passes nearby or glances in my direction that I'm pregnant so that they take the proper precautions with my care. It is surprisingly easy to reveal this information to total strangers, far easier than explaining things to acquaintances around town, or even to friends. I'm finding it cathartic to share what I consider my secrets with the staff, knowing I won't ever have to see these people again. Plus, they are bound by the Health Insurance Portability and Accountability Act (HIPAA) Privacy Rule not to blab.

The orderlies simply smile and nod, sometimes acknowledging me with an "Okay, Miss," after realizing I am being informative and not combative. The nurses display only minimal interest as they scurry past me or stop to take my vital signs again. However, the anesthesiologist, a small, bony woman with a hippie vibe, pauses to discuss this finding further.

"Oh, wow. I'll definitely keep that in mind. How far along are you?" She's not backing out of the surgery it seems, which is comforting.

"About six weeks, I think." I look at Grant. "Sounds about right," he agrees following a short pause, probably to do some quick math.

"Alright." She jots something down on a small notepad pulled from the breast pocket of her blue scrubs. "You and the baby might or might not be sharing a blood supply by now, but either way, it shouldn't be a problem."

I smile at her, admiring both her long dark braid and her confidence. "Thank you," I say.

A moment later, Dr. Conle walks in and lets me know that everything will be fine today. Did he make a point of saying 'today' to avoid any responsibility regarding my fate after discharge, or am I reading into that?

Three young men in scrubs then walk into the room and surround my bed. One is especially cute, despite his blue bouffant cap. Is this how it feels to be Madonna? Whatever has been dripping into my veins through the IV must be starting to take effect because I know I should be nervous that they are manipulating my bed and doing what feels like kicking it, but I can't seem to care. "What are you doing?" I ask one of them calmly. *Too* calmly.

"We're taking you to the O.R., ma'am," says the not as cute one. Wait, no, he is cute. *Ma'am?* Damn. I shouldn't be surprised by this address, but it's a little more painful when it comes from a guy in what looks to be his 20's. Call one of those orderlies in here so I can be called 'Miss' again! I feel the bed start to move and reach for Grant's hand. I hold it for as long as he is allowed to walk next to me. But then we reach the point where we must go down our separate hallways—his leading back to the waiting area and mine to the place where I hope my boob will be made cancer-free. "I love you," he says. "I love you, too," I say and bite my lip, feeling the urge to cry and giggle all at once.

He lets go of my hand and I am wheeled into a brightly lit room, my bed placed parallel to another one that is under some super-bright lights. Everyone is shuffling around me, their surgical shoe covers making scraping noises on the hard, shiny floor. They are all so close. The handrails are lowered and then it feels like a tug-of-war has ensued with the sheet beneath me, like it's being pulled tight. What is happening? "On three," I hear and glance around at the personnel surrounding my bed, each focused on his section of responsibility. "One…two…three." On three, the sheet is lifted with me in it as I am quickly and gently transferred to the operating table. Dr. Conle and the anesthesiologist are near me. There is a gas mask placed over my face. "Breathe deeply," a female voice says.

That's the last thing I remember before I wake up in the recovery room to find Mom and Grant in chairs beside my bed. "Hi," I say groggily. "How did it go?" Grant looks up from his laptop and smiles at me.

"Dr. Conle said it went very well."

"Great." Did the tiny life inside me wake up, too? "I'm so glad it's done."

The curtain slides partially open and a plump, friendly-looking nurse is walking toward me. She must have heard our voices. I attempt to sit up, but as soon as I'm upright I feel dizzy. And then I'm overcome by nausea and there's nothing I can do but grab the little pink kidney bean shaped tray with my free toiletries in it and throw up. I didn't even have time to dump out the free toiletries first. Shoot.

I *hate* throwing up. When there's a barfing scene in a movie I have to close my eyes and cover my ears, like some people do when there's a scene with graphic violence. But even the words—barf, vomit, *ralph*, ralph is the worst for sure—make me want to do that very thing. And now I've just done it for real in front of others. But neither Grant nor the nurse seems offended, or at least they're good at hiding it. The nurse takes the sullied tray and begins to clean me up without missing a beat. "I'm so sorry," I offer apologetically.

"It's okay, sweetie, just lie back down."

I relax into a comfortable recline, somewhat embarrassed. I need to overcome this aversion somehow. Recoiling upon hearing the word 'upchuck' is definitely *not* badass.

I leave the hospital with all sorts of instructions about how to care for the thin yet repugnant tube that is coming out of a hole below my armpit. There is a clear silicone bulb on the end of this tube about the size of a mini bagel. Four times a day the bulb needs to be emptied through the small opening on the top of it. When not being emptied, it is plugged up with its attached stopper. It is already full of bloody fluid by the time we get home. "That's so disgusting," I tell Grant, suppressing a gag.

"It's not as bad as I thought," he says, squeezing the fluid into the measuring cup they gave us. It gurgles and gasps

toward the end, like the last bit of sunblock being forced out
of the bottle.

Sunblock. I was in line to buy some at CVS eleven and
a half years ago when I looked to my left and noticed I was
standing next to a tall, attractive golden-haired guy. He was
buying a card. I became suddenly self-conscious because he
was cute and I hadn't bothered to put on make-up or even
bathe that day. In fact, I had just finished a workout. God, I
hope I don't smell, I thought, pushing a lock of still-sweaty
hair out of my eyes and managing a surreptitious whiff
inside my heavy down coat. I focused my scrutiny back to
the bottle of sunscreen in my hand, studying the ingredi-
ents printed on the back in miniscule letters.

"I bet you're going someplace better than here." I looked
up to see the cute guy I was attempting to ignore waiting
for my response.

"Uh, oh, right," I said as I glanced out the storefront
window and saw the snow falling heavily. "Miami. For
spring break."

He held my gaze and I tried my best not to blush. I
nodded my head during the short awkward silence that
followed. I couldn't have worn just a little concealer today?
"My name's Grant," he offered, extending his hand for me
to shake. Sparks. Definitely sparks. I could practically see
them shoot out of our clasped hands.

When I saw Grant enter the Tufts University gym a
week later, I got butterflies in my stomach. Wait, what was
I doing? I had a boyfriend already, but one that had yet to
cause a single butterfly to flap a wing. Truthfully, I *had* been
reevaluating our relationship and it wasn't looking good.
Plus, he lived so far away...

I deliberately avoided looking into Grant's eyes, a repeat

of the drugstore trick, which hadn't worked then, but I couldn't think of anything else to do. How would I feel if he didn't remember me? How would I handle it if he did? When I looked up from my stationary bike, there he was, settling his tall, athletic build onto the bike next to mine. The butterflies sped up. He socialized for a moment with someone riding a bike to his left and then turned toward me.

"Your name is Stephanie, right? We met at the drugstore last week. How was Miami?" I looked over at him. His eyes were golden, like his hair. My face felt hot.

Grant and I conversed easily for the next few minutes and came to realize we had met before. It was in Hermosa Beach, California, two years prior. We had chatted briefly on a friend's balcony, and I remembered knowing back then he was just my type, with all-American WASP good looks and a liberal perspective. We'd both inquired afterward about each other with our friends, but neither of our friends had followed up and we hadn't seen each other since. And then there we were—in a CVS in Boston, our handshake restoring a lost connection.

I returned from CVS to my small apartment near campus feeling light, like something good had just happened to me, something full of promise. When Grant called the next day to ask me out, those butterflies started fluttering again. I liked hearing his voice on the other end; I loved that he hadn't waited the requisite 72 hours to call; and yet I responded to his invitation with "No, I can't."

"No?" he sounded surprised. Of course he was surprised. We hit it off so well the day before, acknowledging a shared memory, reestablishing a bond, being blown away by the sheer serendipity of finding each other again.

"The thing is," I closed my eyes, grimaced. Oh, this was

so difficult, but it had to be done. "I have a boyfriend." Shoot. It was out there. I probably blew my second chance with this guy. "I'm sorry I didn't tell you before. But really, I'm just not good at the dishonest cheating thing."

"Cheating?" he responded. "Who said you'd be cheating? We could just spend time together as friends, you know. The fact that we met again after all this time is just too weird for us not to hang out in some capacity." Ah, sweet justification.

Yes, I fell for it. I knew I was on a slippery slope, but I did it anyway. Grant and I went out a few times "as friends," with me reminding him of this status whenever he would try to hold my hand or our hug goodbye would linger a little too long. But then he took me to a dance that his program hosted each year. I almost backed out of going with him that very day because I knew I was getting in too deep. I liked him *a lot*. "We're still just going to this thing as friends," I reminded him for the thousandth time.

"Absolutely."

"Okay." I curled my hair and wore a new dress and dabbed on some deliciously scented perfume.

That night, Grant literally swept me off my feet, gliding us around the floor like Patrick Swayze and Jennifer Gray at the end of *Dirty Dancing*. Okay, maybe not that dramatically, and he didn't lift me over his head, but we did dance, talk, and laugh for hours. There was no turning back. My roommate had already informed me that I would be an insane moron not to pursue this relationship. "I'm sorry," she told me. "But no two people look at each other that way who should just stay friends."

The next day I broke up with my boyfriend over the phone. It's not the most respectful way to break up with someone, but I didn't have much of a choice being that he lived in Kentucky. Plus, I desperately wanted to move on to begin what I hoped would be a very significant portion of my life with Grant. I ended up spending an extra year in Boston to be with him while he finished his program at The Fletcher School of Law and Diplomacy, breaking one of the pinky swearing promises my girlfriends and I had made which specifically stated never staying or moving anywhere for a man. But Grant wasn't just a man. He was the right man. A really good guy, and I wasn't about to let him go again. To me, he was the perfect blend of rugged and intellectual. He could catch and gut a salmon by day, thanks to his outdoorsy Pacific Northwest upbringing, and read to me from the collections of Pablo Neruda by night. We found the same things funny, we quoted the same movies, and when one night he brought some ice cream to my apartment and I said, "Thank you, Easter Bunny," he flapped his arms like wings and squawked, "Bawk, bawk" without hesitation, I knew he was The One. He made me feel beautiful and smart and spunky. It was simple. We belonged together. It was fate, and that was that.

And now this is this. I watch Grant as he makes the first entry onto the Fluid Output Chart, carefully holding the cup up to the light to get an accurate measurement, and then writing it down. "I love you," I say, knowing he understands I mean it more at this moment than ever before, even if I don't say those words exactly. He looks over at me. "I love you, too."

I resent the symbiotic relationship I need to maintain with this 'pit drain.' I hate the thing and yet I have to keep it safe from harm so that it can do its job. It can't get wet in the shower so I need to sheathe it in a Ziploc bag and hold it away from the water each time I bathe. It gets its own carrying pouch the rest of the time, which I wear around my neck like I would a passport. Of course a passport means potential freedom and excitement, whereas this thing provides neither. It's more of a noose. It's always there, literally attached to me and in need of accommodation. Maybe I'll name it Kuato, after that revolting little mutant baby growing out of that guy's torso in *Total Recall*.

Two days following the surgery, it is time to remove the surgical dressing. I am so afraid of what I might find once my breast is uncovered that I keep entering and leaving and reentering the bathroom without actually touching the bandages. I eventually begin the process. It takes me about a half hour to complete because following the slow, shaky removal of each square layer of gauze — and there are many formidable layers — I need to sit down, catch my breath and wipe the sweat off my palms and upper lip. You'd think I'd undergone total facial reconstruction the way I am approaching this.

When the bandages are completely shed, my skin finally exposed, the damage doesn't look nearly as bad as I thought it would. No frightening disfigurement or oozing open flesh wounds. There is a slightly puckered three-inch reddish, purplish line along the top of my breast from my armpit toward my sternum and maybe my boob looks just a tiny bit flatter than before in that area. I turn my body to view it from several different angles. I can live with this, I conclude, and throw the pile of crumpled gauze into the trash.

I am very much obsessed with checking my underwear for evidence of a miscarriage. So far, nothing indicates that the baby didn't make it. It's encouraging that I still have morning sickness, but I choose to proceed with caution. I won't let my body fool me again. I am so preoccupied with my internal emotional warfare and my bandage and pit drain drama I forget that at some point during this past week my lymph nodes were tested for the spread of cancer. A pathologist somewhere has probably determined at what 'stage' I am. I don't know all the details on cancer staging, but I know that I am obviously not Stage 0. Stage I is the best I can hope for and I think Stage IV could mean I need to review my life insurance policy.

"I'm scared," I tell Grant on our way to the post-op appointment. "The results Dr. Conle gives us could mean everything, you know? It's one thing to try to keep the pregnancy if I'm Stage I, but anything beyond that might mean we can't. Plus…I could be d…"

"I know, hon," Grant cuts me off before I get too worked up, "but you're going to be fine."

God, I hope he's right. But it's too late. I *am* worked up, my thoughts jumping years ahead, and I'm imagining Grant remarried and I'm already starting to feel jealous and angry. I turn to him and frown, imagining Ethan being raised by the new yoga-instructor/PhD wife. "What?" he asks, looking over at me after we park the car. He appears puzzled by my expression.

I'm nearly jumping out of my skin as Dr. Conle and an intern I don't know come into the room with my pathology results. I hold my breath as Dr. Conle scans the report. He leans against the counter and moves his finger down the first page. "Okay," he begins, "we took out 17 lymph nodes, and it says…let me see here, okaaaay." He flips the pages back and forth on the clipboard, searching for the right section. I have yet to exhale and my heart is pounding. *Find the answer, hurry up!* The next second takes at least four minutes, enough time for me to break into a cold sweat.

"Alright, here we go…cancer was found in…o out of 17 lymph nodes." He looks up at me. I breathe again and close my eyes. Dr. Conle walks over to hug me and so does Grant. Random but smiley intern gives me the thumbs up. I give him one right back.

I then proudly produce my drainage chart, like a kid showing her parents a good report card, and wait for review and praise. Dr. Conle studies it a moment, nods his head in approval and opens a drawer under the counter. I hope he's going for the pit-drain-removing instrument. He takes out a pair of scissors, but maybe that's it? He comes back over to me. "Lift your arm, please," he requests.

I try, but it hurts to lift it. My shoulder is so stiff from non-use that I can make only a little space for him to reach in to clip the suture that's holding the drain in place. I read online this part is not a big deal so I'm not expecting any…

"Ow! Son of a *bitch*," I fail to contain the outburst as a sharp pain shoots up into my armpit and down my left side. Internet liars!

"Sorry, not you," I frown as he puts a Band-Aid over the small hole that is left behind from the tube's removal. But my discomfort is quickly eclipsed by the realization of not having to deal with Kuato any longer. He has been snipped from my life, and seeing the empty pouch in which he used to reside crumpled on a chair in the corner makes me giddy. That and remembering that the cancer has most likely not spread to my other body parts.

"I'm going to write you up a referral for PT," Dr. Conle says.

"Physical therapy?" I take it he noticed my pathetically small range of motion when I tried to lift my arm. "No, thank you, I can get full range back on my own. I used to be an occupational therapist, you know," I inform him, leaving out the fact that I haven't actually worked in this profession for nearly a decade. "I can do it," I assure him. Where *did* I put those handouts on finger wall climbs?

According to the pathology report, the tumor was 1.8 cm. I imagine a smallish black mass squirming around in the lab screaming with its little demon mouth while pathologists hold it down to get an accurate measurement. Are tumors black? Probably not. I only know how it appeared on the ultrasound screen. However, this infernal little beast is out, and because it is under 2 cm and was thankfully caught before spreading its fiendishness to the lymph nodes, I am deemed Stage I. Considering my new standards, this is really great news.

On our way home, however, as I scan the copy of the pathology report that was given to us, a certain phrase jumps out at me—"extensive cancerization of the lobules." I know that lobules are the milk-producing glands of the breast. And mine had *extensive cancerization*? That's a phrase that I could spend the rest of my days trying to forget, but it will never be erased completely from my brain. Those words will haunt me. How did cancer have the time to make itself so extensive in there, so vast? I get the feeling my mind is going to take far longer than my body to clean up from all of this.

CHAPTER 8

"Hey, Soul Sister" – Train

There are still some serious loose ends that needed tying off, and now that the surgery is done, we can focus on them. First and foremost, I need to find an oncologist. Second, I think I need to find a new OB/Gyn. I am simply not convinced that Dr. Hogan is on board with my plan to keep the baby and go through cancer treatment at the same time, and I can't shake the feeling I am a burden to him as he continually brings up insurance coverage concerns. He's been accommodating to this point, I'll give him that. Of course, I haven't given him much choice, just barging into his office lately. But the man *never* even smiles at me and right now I really need every bit of encouragement I can get.

The oncologist is top priority, though, because I have no one yet and I need to move on with the next phase of treatment. One woman's name has come up a few times over the course of our research from people who have either been treated for cancer or know someone who has — Dr. Lois Sung. She works at City of Hope, the same place as one of my new favorite people, Dr. Santos.

Grant suggests we bypass Dr. Sung's schedulers and instead calls Dr. Santos directly. "Remember? My wife's the pregnant one?" Grant asks him on the phone. "You mentioned a Dr. Sung at our last visit. We'd like to meet with her." Sidestepping conventional appointment-making protocol definitely works in our favor because within two days, we receive a call from Dr. Sung's office. I doubt that would have happened nearly so quickly had I called and tearfully begged a scheduler for top priority.

In Dr. Sung's waiting room, I shuffle through the magazines on the table next to me, longing for a mindless tabloid to provide some distraction. Hmm, *Cancer Today*, and *Cure*. No, no, not interested. I stand up and walk across the room where there is a clear plastic rack hung vertically on the wall. I scan the glossy covers there. Not one bit of fluff. It seems the only subscriptions available have to do with cancer. Why in the world would I want to read about cancer? I'm certainly not interested in other types. I'm not about to flip through the pages of *Cancer Today* looking for ideas, like I'm at the hair salon. "That's the last thing I need," I mumble to no one in particular. Continuing my search, I dig deeper into one of the slots and pull out an issue, hoping to see the word *People* printed across the top. Instead, this one has a garish pink ribbon taking up nearly the entire cover. Oh, that's right, it's October.

"It's Breast Cancer Awareness Month," I direct my raised voice to Grant, who's sitting in a chair across the room. He looks up and I tap at the ribbon. He raises his eyebrows and says just what I'm thinking, "Timely." A couple of the other patients glance up at me. I make eye contact with one and tap the pink ribbon again. She rolls her eyes. Was that a nod to our solidarity or is she telling me to sit down and shut up? I don't know.

Eventually, we are called out of the waiting area and escorted to a private exam room to wait for Dr. Sung. I change into a hospital gown and 15 nervous minutes later

Dr. Sung enters, bursting into the room, right hand extended for greeting. She introduces herself, hugs me and then asks if I brought any ultrasound pictures.

I am positively stunned. Is this woman for real? Did she just ask me for photos? Not to mention this is the second hug from a doctor I've received in this place, and I've only met with two doctors!

I study her a moment before responding to her request. She is a small but sturdy Asian woman with puffy, feathered shoulder length hair. Her mouth is smiling sincerely but her eyes convey an intensity that could bore through steel. Her confidence and intelligence are so overt that I don't know whether to be impressed or intimidated. I suppose I'm both, which is an acceptable way to feel about someone who might have my life in her hands.

"Um, I do have some," I answer and reach into my ever-growing file folder to pull out the photos. I hand them to her. Dr. Sung studies the image of the miniscule grain of rice whose heartbeat is 'quite strong.'

"Aw, how wonderful," Dr. Sung says after a moment, handing the pictures back to me. I glance over at Grant in disbelief. Did she just say *wonderful*?

"You did read my chart, right?" I ask suspiciously while searching for the inevitable change of expression and demeanor as she glances through my paperwork.

"Yes," she nods and continues smiling at me. "Based on everything I've read, I strongly believe that I can save both you and your baby." I stare at her blankly. "What do you think of that?" she asks gently.

"Good," is all I can squeak out before I begin to sniffle and my eyes fill with tears of relief, joy, and trepidation.

Dr. Sung gets me a Kleenex and then goes on to describe

the treatment plan she has in mind, should I decide to choose her for my oncologist. Should I? I'm already writing her flowery thank you cards in my head and naming this baby Lois, regardless of its gender.

"Um, yes, I believe you are the doctor for me," I say as I dab my eyes and blow my nose into the Kleenex. Dr. Sung suggests we begin with four rounds of chemotherapy, a fairly standard cocktail of Adriamycin and Cytoxan, to be received through an IV once every three weeks for four sessions. Both of these drugs, as harsh and toxic as they are, have been given to pregnant women in their second and third trimesters and have miraculously not affected the fetuses.

"But why? How is it that the fetus isn't harmed?" I ask, recalling how with Ethan I shunned lunchmeat, brie cheese and sushi. I didn't dare touch a cat, not trusting its association with its own litter box and the possible toxoplasmosis that could be passed on to the innocent fetus should the cat decide to claw me for no reason. In hindsight, I might have been a bit paranoid.

"Well, there really haven't been formal studies on this yet, but we know the placenta functions as a filter, protecting the baby from certain things by not letting them pass through," Dr. Sung explains. "It seems as though the particular drugs you'd be administered do not penetrate the placenta, whereas other drugs and toxins might."

"So I still shouldn't take an aspirin, but I can go through chemo?"

"Crazy, isn't it?"

"Completely," I confirm, taking it all in. But somehow Dr. Sung's explanation, while making no sense, makes all the sense in the world. If the placenta protects the baby, the baby is protected—simple. And yet baffling.

Dr. Sung further illustrates the treatment plan. I would take a break following the initial four rounds of chemo, allowing blood cell counts to return to normal as chemo often alters them. I can give birth more safely if my red blood cells are 'within normal limits.' I realize up to this point I haven't imagined actually delivering a baby, so I'm a bit shocked to hear her refer to this event. I try to concentrate on the rest of the procedure, but I essentially tune out after Dr. Sung says "give birth." I hope Grant is taking notes. I hear the words 'Taxol' and 'radiation', but as those will all occur *after* the baby's arrival, I am incapable of processing what they mean for me right now.

"It sounds like you've done this before. *Have* you done this before?" I ask, returning to the conversation and realizing this probably should have been my first question for her.

"Yes, I have," Dr. Sung smiles.

"And?" I ask, both wary and hopeful.

"That patient visited me just recently with her daughter who is now four. She brought her in to show off her tiger Halloween costume — the daughter's, that is."

I imagine a grinning woman holding the paw/hand of a tiny fluffy tiger/girl and feel myself well up again. Could that actually be me someday showing off my little trick-or-treater? I want it to be more than anything but I'm having trouble conceiving a similar scene with me in it.

"When would we start?" I ask.

"About four weeks from now would be a good time to begin treatment. I'd like for the fetus be further along in its development before we begin."

"Can we wait that long without putting Stephanie at significantly greater risk?" Grant asks.

Dr. Sung assures us that it won't make a difference. She

says in all likelihood the cancer has not spread. Grant flashes me a quick, relieved grin.

"Then why do I need chemo at all, really?" I ask, as if this will shed new light on my situation and a surprised, delighted Dr. Sung will answer, "Well, I hadn't really thought about that. You're right, you don't!"

"Because your cancer type is very aggressive and you are young. There is the slight chance that some cancer cells could have broken off from the tumor and escaped into your bloodstream."

"So I have to go through chemo because of the possibility of a rogue cell or two?" I ask, still frustrated that she didn't change her mind and tell me I am free to go and live my life without a flashing neon 'Coming soon: Chemotherapy' sign looming in the distance.

"Yes, but those rogue cells, if left unchecked, could do serious damage and make all the difference."

"You mean they could kill me," I respond.

"It's possible," says Dr. Sung. I suspect the answer is really more of a 'Yes!' but I can tell this woman is an eternal optimist.

"Okay, okay, I know I have to do it," I relent. "I just don't want to."

"I have yet to meet a patient who does."

We all gather around the small calendar on her desk and come up with January 15, 2008.

"Will I lose my hair?" I ask.

"Yes," she says.

I knew the answer to that question before I asked it, but for some reason I'm holding on to the fantasy that my follicles have super-strength and that by the end of January I will not resemble Bruce Willis.

"At least you won't have to shave for a while," Dr. Sung says.

"What do you mean?"

"I think she means you don't just lose the hair on your head," Grant grasps.

"What? Everything goes? Armpits? Eyebrows and eyelashes, too?"

"Possibly."

"Even down there?" I point girlishly to my nether regions.

"Even down there."

I don't know why I never thought of these areas as being potentially bald, too. I really don't want to lose my eyebrows and eyelashes. I doubt Dr. Sung has met a patient who wants *that*, either. Should it happen I imagine I'll resemble a fat pink mole rat. Strange. But the legs, armpits and pubic hair? Not so bad, really. My showers will be done in record time.

"I have one more question," I say. I probably will have a million more questions, but this is the only one I can think of now.

"Will I get Chemo Lite?"

Dr. Sung and Grant look at me, confused.

"I mean, I assume the treatment is somewhat watered down because of the pregnancy, right?"

Dr. Sung shakes her head. "No," she responds. "You will get the regular dosage. It's actually based on a person's weight, so technically it might be more for you than it would normally be, should you gain weight due to the baby."

"Wow, okay," I take a deep breath. Her answer scares me. I imagine the placenta meaning well, but becoming overloaded with toxins until it just can't hold out anymore. *But she's done this before*, I remind myself, *and everything was okay*. Still. Frightening, very frightening.

As we make our way out of City of Hope to the parking lot, I am feeling rather confident in myself.

"I think I can handle all this," I proclaim, nodding my head in self-agreement.

"I know you can," Grant says as he opens the car door for me.

But as we drive away from the facility, with each mile separating us further from Dr. Sung and her self-assuredness, my confidence starts to teeter. I keep this waning sensation to myself because I don't want to ruin anything for Grant. He seems to really share Dr. Sung's positive outlook regarding the ultimate outcome.

Should I believe everything she just told me? Am I really protecting this baby by keeping it? Should I also consider the possibility that both Grant and this very well respected doctor are a bit delusional and I am the voice of reason?

The seed of skepticism I personally planted into my brain takes root overnight and by the next day has blossomed into panic and a decision to withdraw from yesterday's plan. *I can't do this.* And then I start to cry and yell out loud.

"I CAN'T DO THIS!! I was crazy to try to take both of these things on. And now I won't be just crazy, I'll be fat and bald, too!"

Grant is at work, so Mom enters the room to find me talking and sometimes yelling to no one. "I have to terminate this baby," I tell her in conclusion and then repeat the phrase over and over, as I begin to pace around the room, pressing my fingers to my temples. Why is Mom looking at me like that?

"Steph! Are you okay? What are you doing?" she asks. I turn on her.

"I'll tell you what I'm doing," I say in a voice I don't totally recognize. "I'm imagining endless doctor's appointments, constant needle pokes, which I despise, no guarantee that this baby will be okay, and it would be all *my* fault if it's not, and a perpetual feeling of nausea, first from this," I point with intensity to my stomach, "and then from chemo because of *this*." I point now to my left boob. "And what? I'm supposed to go to chemotherapy with a big old belly and everyone staring at me like I've lost my mind because I clearly have? Huh?" I shrug and hold up my clammy palms to her, waiting for an answer. Mom opens her mouth to speak, but I don't give her the chance.

I push past her out of the room to go lock myself in the bathroom. What was I thinking? I can't handle this. This bathroom feels very small.

I open the door and take off down the hallway for the den. I pick up the phone and heatedly dial Dr. Hogan's office to schedule an abortion. Closed for lunch? Damn! I slam the phone down and dash for the kitchen, over to the drawer where Mom keeps the phone books. I lug one out, drop it onto the floor and flip it open. I am on a quest for the number to Planned Parenthood. "They'll help me," I mutter as I run my finger up and down the pages, scanning through the 'P's.'

I am still squatting on the kitchen floor with the phone book when Jenn shows up. "Steph?" I look up for a second and then back down to the book to continue my search. When did Mom call *her*?

"It's too much! I've changed my mind!" I assert loudly. Jenn begins slowly walking toward me.

"What are you doing?" she asks. I don't look up this time. Instead, I straighten my arm out sideways toward her, giving the Stop Right There sign with my hand.

If this were a movie, this would be the part when my normally composed character has become unhinged by an unfortunate circumstance and begins brandishing a gun threateningly saying, "Stand back or I'll shoot! Don't make me do it!" Jenn is the nice cop, trying to talk me down before I do anything I'll regret. She steps closer to me.

"I'm going to take the phone book now," she warns, gently but firmly.

That is just what the nice cop would say! Okay, it's official. I've lost my mind. I don't fight her as she closes the book gently and pushes it over the hard tile away from me.

I face her. "I can't do this," I whisper. She hugs me and then puts a hand on each of my shoulders and looks me in the eyes.

"I understand," she says. "It's a lot." I start to cry. "But if anyone can do this, you can. It won't be easy, but I know you can do it. I know you want this baby." I *do*. She continues, "And I think you two are going to make it through this together. You are so much stronger than you realize." I stare back at her for a moment and then look down at the floor. I feel my eyes welling up yet again.

"Oh yeah, real strong, true grace under fire," I say, wiping my tears on my sleeve. "I just had a complete breakdown. A complete breakdown, when less than 24 hours ago, I felt okay. How do I know that won't keep happening?"

"Maybe it will," she responds with a small shrug, "and then Mom will call me and I'll be here again." I look back up at her. I take a deep breath and look at mom. She smiles, too, and nods, reaching for a Kleenex.

Later, as I'm changing into my pajamas, I rehash my Morning of Madness to Grant again. I already told him the basics on the phone, but now that Ethan is asleep, I can fill in the gaps.

"You should have seen me, hon, I was like a lunatic. Jenn had to talk me down from the ledge."

"I think you're allowed a meltdown or two."

"Or maybe a hundred," I say.

"Or maybe a hundred," he repeats.

"Yeah, but I came so close to throwing in the towel, to *terminating* the baby," I admit with a shudder.

"I don't think you would have followed through. I mean, if it was really what you wanted, I wouldn't have stopped you, but I don't think it is." He adds, "You are a brave, strong woman."

"I'm not," I assure him. "I'm scared out of my head to do this."

"Being brave doesn't mean you're not scared. Being brave is being scared out of your mind, and doing what you need to do anyway."

Hmmm. How is it that Grant and I are exactly the same age and yet he seems to possess so much more wisdom than I? If he ever switches his sentence structure around I might have to start calling him Yoda.

I put my hand on my belly. "I wish I had a crystal ball so I'd know how this all turns out." And just when I thought I was done with crazy for the day, that's when I feel her.

Not the baby. Grandma June. Grant's Grandma June whom I adored from the moment Grant introduced us ten years back until the day she passed away three years ago. I've thought of her often since then, recalling her short, round shape, her friendly, welcoming face, and her long white hair always pulled back into a low bun. I miss our deep discussions about everything from politics to art, fashion and food. A docent at the Portland Art Museum for years, she was so knowledgeable, so cultured, so open minded and so cool. When I showed her my one and only tattoo, I braced myself for "Why would you do that though? You're 33 already!" Instead, she smiled and said, "Oh, I love it! It's beautiful."

She was an outstanding cook and everyone in the family looked forward to the holiday meals at her house. One of my first Thanksgivings as a Hosford, I told her I came across a turkey recipe that seemed interesting and different. She insisted we try it. I felt so honored that someone with her culinary skills would be open to an impromptu sugges- tion from such a novice as myself, especially for the main dish. Luckily, it turned out well, with a few deft Grandma tweaks (and covert winks in my direction) to prevent it from becoming The Thanksgiving That Stephanie Ruined. But that was Grandma June. *Is* Grandma June?

I don't claim to understand it, but I can *feel* her. She is sitting beside me at this moment with one arm around me, the other hand placed over mine on my belly. "It's okay," I can hear her say gently. "I'm taking care of this baby. She will be fine. Trust."

She? How does Grandma June know it's a she? Wait, I'm open to accepting that Grant's dead grandmother is sitting here with me but I'm questioning her ability to detect the baby's gender? Just go with it, I tell myself. *Please stay with me*, I beg her silently. "Trust," she repeats. *Trust?* Trust whom? Trust what? Why is she being so vague?

And where is Dad, by the way? Why is it Grandma June and not my own dad paying me a visit? I think I know.

I loved my dad. He taught me how to pitch a baseball, throw a football in an impressive spiral, and drive a stick shift, all skills that impressed various boyfriends, although that was probably not Dad's goal. Thanks to him I was the only six-year-old I knew who could sing every word of Don McLean's "American Pie" and The Eagles' "Lyin' Eyes." I have many memories of him pulling into the garage with Fleetwood Mac or Credence Clearwater Revival blasting from within his car, Dad singing even louder than the band.

He was a good man, handsome with his dark hair, blue eyes, and a boyish grin. He was capable of so much fun and humor when he was in a happy mood. But Dad also had a temper that flared unpredictably, a bit too often to qualify him as an overall calming force in my life. So while he has my blessing to visit Ethan someday soon on the soccer field to help him play more aggressively, I think Dad is graciously stepping aside for this, knowing my current circumstance is a better fit for Grandma June.

But then she's gone. It's just me now sitting on the bed, hand still on my stomach. I'm squinting at my reflection, searching for some sign of her, when Grant says, "Come on, get some sleep," as he pats my pillow. Do I tell him what just happened? I open my mouth to begin, but then close it. I don't know why, but I think this is to be kept between Grandma June and me. Plus, I don't want to risk having anyone tell me that it was only my imagination. Even if it was, I need her. The baby needs her. Because along with Dr. Sung, I get the feeling Grandma June just might save us both.

❖

One thing is certain. It's time to make what I view is the biggest decision of my life. I must choose a path and not look back. There can be no more hemming or hawing. No more calls to Planned Parenthood. It's time to "shit or get off the pot" as Mom has so delicately stated when Jenn or I hesitated to make a decision in the past.

In general, I am more comfortable following rules. I typically don't walk across the street when the signal clearly states 'Don't Walk.' I drive within the speed limit. I don't place 15 items on a conveyor belt that is reserved for those with 12 items or less. It's just the way I am.

However, I've made a few choices that might be considered risky by some. I've smoked pot, I have my aforementioned small tattoo, I took a gamble on Grant by moving with him to Brazil. I even once jumped off the top of a considerably large rock into Lake Nacimiento. But this is different. This is relatively uncharted territory by anyone's standards. And this decision affects more than just me. This involves my children. And it cannot be reversed.

The doctors at City of Hope, Grant, Jenn, Mom, my in-laws and the small circle of friends I've told are all behind me if I move forward with the pregnancy. This is an enormous advantage and yet will still require a colossal leap of faith.

"Trust." Grandma June's words echo in my ears. I close my eyes for a moment.

Upon opening them back up, I sit up tall, look at myself in the mirrored closet and take a long, deep breath.

All right. I'm in.

CHAPTER 9

"All Star" – Smash Mouth

As I head into the second trimester, I have a brighter outlook. This may be partly due to the abatement of morning sickness. But I think mostly it has to do with feeling a sense of commitment, of decisiveness. I have given my final answer to the question put forth three months ago: I am not terminating the pregnancy.

Certitude isn't always easy for me. It once took me two years to decide on a bathing suit because of my continuous revisions to the requirements regarding color, coverage, and fabric type. Did I want that little gold ring on each hip? I had trouble coming to a conclusion. I change my hair color about twice a year (something my father-in-law finds entertaining), never quite satisfied with the chosen shade, forever looking back at pictures of my previous color with longing. Not surprisingly, I don't run marathons. I stick to short triathlons because there is no commitment to any one sport for too long. As soon as I start to get bored, then yay, there is a transition to the next leg of the race, and then before monotony can set in, I'm done and on to a big, greasy breakfast.

Along these lines, unless there is a major controversy on which to take a stand, I can usually see both sides of an argument, and be swayed one way or the other depending on my mood. But this is not one of those times. There is from now on only one side of this issue for me. Moving forward, however, will involve an added task: I need to find a new OB/Gyn.

Dr. Hogan does not seem to be moving in any positive

direction on the encouragement/warmth continuum. When I had excitedly told him about the wonderful oncologist I found, he asked me flatly, "And what's so special about her?" A slight burst to my bubble, but I elaborated with how smart and warm and experienced she is. He maintained his stoicism, barely lifting an eyebrow in response. I added, "Actually, she said she called you to chat about me and left a message. Did you talk to her yet?"

"Hmmm, what was her name again?" he asked me.

"Um, Dr. Sung, oncologist at City of Hope..."

"Hmmm, I don't think so, not yet."

You don't *think* so? Exactly how many oncologists call each day to discuss their pregnant patients that you're treating? The deal was really done after our most recent appointment with him when Grant said, "We need to switch doctors because every time I see this guy, I want to punch him in the face." It's time to make a change.

After looking up our provider group in the HMO directory, I find a few specialists listed who are nearby. The first one I call isn't taking new patients, and when I pull the "but I have breast cancer, too" card, they are especially sure they aren't taking new patients. Great, doctors are afraid of me. Perfect. I call the next name on the list. Wrong number... and so is the new number that is given to me by the recorded voice. Moving right along.

Next in the book is a Dr. Mitchell. I dial and the receptionist answers. Yes, he is taking new patients, she informs me. She sounds friendly. "Okay, here's the deal..." and I explain my situation.

"Dios mio! I'll have the doctor call you."

Right. I give her my number, hang up and resume my search.

To my utter surprise, Dr. Mitchell calls me back that very day. "So I'm told you are pregnant and have been diagnosed with breast cancer."

"That's right," I say.

"I'd like you to come in with your significant other, if you have one, and meet with me so we can go over a treatment plan for you."

"Really? I didn't scare you away?" I ask, astonished. He laughs slightly.

"No, I can handle this."

I'm really developing an appreciation for over-confident doctors.

I break the news the next day to my now former OB — or rather, to his receptionist. I chicken out at first and tell her that it's all because of insurance and switching groups, and you know how it goes.

"Well, Dr. Hogan is in that group, too," she says. Shoot.

"Oh, hmmm…well…fine, the truth is that I am just not comfortable with Dr. Hogan and feel that my new OB is a better fit for me." Of course, I've yet to encounter Dr. Mitchell in person, so at this point I can only hope this is true.

"Oh. Who is it?"

Not that it's her business, but I reveal, "Dr. Mitchell."

"Oh, he's wonderful." Phew.

We meet with Dr. Mitchell and I like him immediately. "Welcome," he says as we enter his office. He looks to be in his mid to late 40's, tall and gangly, with exceptionally large hands and a somewhat aquiline nose. He is like a large but friendly bird. His office is neither uncomfortably neat, like Dr. Milbrook's, the oncologist who barely spoke to me, nor noticeably messy like Dr. Hogan's, which often gave the impression that he was already overwhelmed, even before I arrived to aggravate him. He and Grant seem to hit it off, digressing into a discussion involving their mutual appreciation of fine watches. This is nice because now I don't have to stress about Grant's potential arrest for assaulting my OB. Of course, Dr. Mitchell is about a foot taller than Dr. Hogan, even a couple of inches taller than Grant, and looks like he might be capable of putting up a fight. I consider this a plus.

Dr. Mitchell is smart, Caltech smart, I notice as I scan the various framed achievements on his walls. He explains that he will monitor me in the same way any 'normal' pregnancy would be but he will also send me to a perinatologist for extra examination. Due to my "maturish age" for pregnancy, as Dr. Mitchell puts it, and the chemotherapy drugs to be received, I am considered 'at risk' by my insurance carrier and therefore entitled to extra help. The perinatologist, an expert in fetal development, will perform several ultrasounds along the way.

"Most likely, the baby will be delivered early and by C-section," he tells us, "according to my research."

"Thank you for researching my case," I say, impressed that he looked into things before he even met me, although I already knew those particulars due to my own obsessive investigations. Delivering by Cesarean will be a new experience for me, but I have yet to find something about this enterprise that isn't new.

I tell Dr. Mitchell I won't let him down.

"You'll see," I say, remembering my first pregnancy and how well I took care of myself and exercised all the way up until the 38th week, until I could barely fit in the car to drive to the gym. "I'll be a great patient. I eat well, exercise all the time, and take my vitamins. I mean, before this whole cancer thing, I was one of the healthiest people I knew." I smile confidently, pausing for him to tell me how impressed he is.

"I'm sure you were," he says, smiling back at me. "But during chemo, it's not a good idea to elevate your heart rate too much."

"So I can't exercise?"

"Not so much," he says. Oh no.

I don't want to throw a big fit as it would be correctly interpreted as not having my priorities straight. However, I can't help but feel a bit panicked because working out, whether it is outside in the fresh air or inside a loud, sweaty gym, is when I find my true happy place. I love when adrenaline flows, my music pumps in my ears, and I transcend the stressors in my life, becoming one with the treadmill, the bike, the trail, the weights. How am I going to transcend *now*?

"What am I supposed to do?" I ask. "How am I supposed to keep my sanity through all of this?"

"You can meditate," he offers up sincerely.

Meditate? I don't know exactly what that involves, but I'm fairly sure it includes a lot of sitting still and thinking, something in which I have very little interest. I don't want to think anymore, I just want to do. I want to do so that I can be done. I need distractions. If anything, I probably need a *more* complicated, *more* active life so I that I don't have time to dwell on any one nerve-racking aspect of it.

CHAPTER 10

"Lightning Crashes" – Live

Dr. Santos recommends I receive genetics counseling. This will likely include a blood test that will let me know if I carry a genetic mutation, which could have caused the cancer. After making an appointment with the genetics department at City of Hope, I am sent a very long and detailed questionnaire regarding my medical history as well as that of my family. The 'Personal History' questions are quick and easy to answer because up until now I didn't have much of a medical history. I suppose that has been changed for good...or I should say, for bad.

The 'Family History' section is proving a bit of a challenge, however. I can fill out the areas regarding Mom, Dad and Jenn, but beyond that I realize I have no idea if other family members ever had cancer. I have one remaining grandparent, my Grandma Irene (a.k.a. Bubbe) who lives a few miles away. Mom finally convinced her a few years ago to move to California from New Jersey so she wouldn't have to spend another whole winter inside her stiflingly overheated apartment for fear of slipping on ice and breaking a hip if she ventured outdoors. She actually did slip on ice a few times out there, the worst fall resulting in a broken nose, which to Grandma Irene was probably more serious than a broken hip because it involved her pretty face about which she *still* gets compliments. She is 94 years old, has never been sick, and attributes this to a hefty intake of daily vitamins and apple cider vinegar. None of Bubbe's teeth are her own, but regardless, it's hard to deny that she has been doing *something* right.

However, she is less than helpful regarding the family tree, insisting that no one on her side of the family ever had cancer. Whether that's entirely true or not is unclear as I'm not sure Bubbe would admit to such a stigma, as she still whispers the c-word rather than say it aloud. Mom doesn't know of anyone on her side either, which is not a huge surprise since her main source of information would be Bubbe. Hence, the only pattern emerging so far is an abundance of blank lines on this tree I'm supposed to complete for the genetics department.

As for Dad's side, Mom says neither of my grandparents had cancer. "There might have been an aunt though," Mom says, "Your dad's Aunt Pauline died young and I seem to recall it was from cancer."

"How young?" I ask.

"Um, 38 maybe?" Mom says and immediately gives me a nervous look and I know we are both thinking the same thing—I turn 38 next month.

I call my dad's brother, Uncle Mike, in New Jersey to interview him about what he can add to my genetics inquest. He says he doesn't know of anyone except for the aunt Mom mentioned.

"She was your Grandpa Ben's sister, Pauline," he says. He thinks she maybe, perhaps, possibly, might have died from breast cancer in her late 30's... "But maybe that was cancer of her uterus," he adds helpfully.

My less than complete and quite possibly inaccurate family health history pages leave me wondering whether essentially no one in my family had any connection to breast cancer, or if they were just unwilling to admit to one. But

I fill out the paperwork as much as I can, and turn it in on the day of my appointment.

Numbers are run based on the given information and somehow whoever makes the calculations still manages to come up with a 25% chance that I carry the gene.

"The blood test will tell us for sure," says the geneticist, Dr. Jordan, during my consultation. She is a tall beautiful black woman in high heels and Prada eyeglasses. "Do you want to be tested?"

It's another needle, another chance to wait and worry about results, but yes, I need to know this. I need some answers.

"Yes, please," I respond. "Does that happen today?"

"Sure," she says, "I'll have the nurse come do that now."

She sticks her head out the door and asks someone I can't see to come draw my blood when they get a chance. I begin to roll up my left shirtsleeve in anticipation, but then remember that I am no longer allowed to get blood draws on the left side. Now that so many lymph nodes have been removed from that armpit, all needles must invade the right arm instead. Any bacteria or disruption in blood flow on the left could potentially cause my arm to swell up for weeks. Even blood pressure has to be taken on the right side only. Jeez. I roll down my sleeve, pull up the other one and look at my forearm. Shoot, how is anyone going to get blood from these spindly little veins? The good, juicy one is on the left.

"So, what if I test positive for this breast cancer gene?" I ask. "What does that mean?"

A woman enters the room with what looks like a small lunch cart, but in fact it carries only blood test related items. She sets up the familiar collection tubes, small but hated needle and so forth, ties a tourniquet around my right biceps and cleans the target area with an alcohol wipe. Her fingers press on my forearm and I know what's coming. I look away.

"Well," Dr. Jordan says, "it could mean your sister might want to be tested, and your mom. Your sister's daughter could be affected as well as your own children."

I wince as the needle pokes into my right arm. I try to maintain focus on what Dr. Jordan is telling me.

"Also," Dr. Jordan adds, "if the results are positive, you might want to consider prophylactic surgery to remove your breast tissue and your ovaries to reduce the chances of future cancers." Oh wow, I've heard of women who do this. Or was that an episode of *Grey's Anatomy*? Regardless, the thought makes me lightheaded as I feel the blood drain from my face. I don't know if it's the blood test or the thought of removing my body parts that's making me feel faint; most likely it's a combination. The needle comes out and a cotton ball with tape over it is placed on my arm.

"Please try not to worry," says Dr. Jordan. "Let's see what the results are first, and then cross those other bridges later."

"Okay," I agree, knowing there is no way I will not worry about this for the next two to three weeks. How is it possible I would not worry?

As I'm leaving, I realize I don't know which test result I prefer. On one hand, if I carry the gene, I would have a reason for why this happened to me, and I would love to be able to blame something for cancer, even if that something was built into my genetic code and is therefore beyond my control. On the other hand, the gene would be incredibly frightening because of what it could mean for my family and all the decisions I would need to make. Christ, there are so many things for me to contemplate and stress over and research and wait for. Will I hit a breaking point? And what will that look like if I do? I wonder if I should be driving as I speed home.

Two weeks later, I get a call from Dr. Jordan. I do *not* carry the gene mutation. As predicted, I am greatly relieved and really confused at the same time.

"Why did this happen then?" I ask her.

She explains that all cancer has genetic components and that some of us are born more predisposed than others to develop it, but what triggered my cancer cells to begin dividing and multiplying could be any combination of many environmental factors. This is very unsatisfying. Does this mean I'll never know? How am I supposed to go through life not knowing what caused this?

I hang up and rack my brain for anything to explain the cancer, some sort of noxious matter I was exposed to or that I ingested repeatedly in the past. Was it all that hairspray I've breathed in during my lifetime? Car exhaust? Second-hand cigarette smoke? Makeup? Body lotion? Smog? Bottled water? Non-bottled water? The occasional red meat? WHAT? WHAT WAS IT? For God's sake, tell me, and I'll stop doing it! In that instant, I get an idea.

I run down the hallway and into the bathroom and madly start throwing away every cosmetic item has the word 'paraben' listed as an ingredient. A friend recently told me parabens are preservatives used in many cosmetics and they might be linked to cancer. It turns out I am trashing essentially every product in the bathroom. I move on to the other bathroom and then delve into my purse. I fill up several small garbage pails with half-full, almost completely full, and even unopened bottles of evil lotion, hair products, and makeup.

I'm no psychologist, but even in the midst of my frenzy, I understand that I am trying to gain some sort of control in my utterly out of control life. Whether or not parabens truly caused my cancer is not the point. I am taking action! By cleaning out those bathroom cabinets, I'm giving myself a fresh start.

Of course, my newfound quest for purity is going to require some funding as now I am left with half a tube of Tom's of Maine all natural toothpaste and a single blush brush made from bamboo.

And I haven't even started with the refrigerator.

CHAPTER 11

"Don't Stop the Music – Rihanna

A couple of days following my beauty product and unwhole-some food purge, my sense of empowerment already waning, I decide to seek out a support group. It is not typically in my nature to share personal business with those outside my family and I've never been masterful at expressing my feelings, but maybe this is what I need. I'm tired of researching organic food, makeup, and shampoo to replace what I threw away, so this might be a welcome new endeavor.

Before acceptance into the group, it is required that I meet with the program director, Judy, for an interview. Is it possible I could be denied entry into a support group? Upon my arrival, I meet Judy, a plump woman with glasses, short curly hair, and no smile. She leads me into a room with a small sofa, a chair, and a television. I sit down on the sofa and a video begins of a woman talking about the day she was diagnosed with cancer, how she handled it, how she broke the news to loved ones, etc. As I wipe away some tears and fidget in my seat, I wonder if Judy, sitting in the chair beside me, is taking mental notes on my response to the video. Did I display too much emotion? Not enough? Why do I even care what Judy thinks? I wish this whole process hadn't been referred to as 'an interview,' because now I'm nervous.

Next is the one-on-one discussion/interview. Judy asks, "How are you dealing with your situation?"

"Well, um, I'm trying my best to multitask, but..."

"How do you feel in general?"

"Um, scared, but starting to be more positive, I think," I say, trailing off a little.

"Do you have a support system outside of this particular center?" she asks while jotting down my previous answer.

"Yes, lucky for me, I do. I have a wonderfully supportive husband, mother, sister…" Judy has yet to look up at me.

"Mmm hmm," she says, scribbling away on her paper. I lean forward and attempt to look at what she is writing but I can't see it clearly. She continues, "Do you fear you might die from cancer?"

"Well, sometimes," I respond, after a pause. She's still not looking at me, even after *that* question?

She asks a few more and then circles back. "Are you afraid of dying from this?" Jesus, what is this woman after? Does she want me to break down in front of her begging for her help? There have been so many meltdowns, so much fear and hopelessness. Well, the fear is still there, but I'm attempting to embrace my recent surge of positivity, thanks to my medical team being in order and my recent visit by Grandma June from the afterlife. I'm finally able to poke my vulnerable head up out of the hole of despair to have a look around, get my bearings. And yet here's Judy, grabbing my ankle from below to yank me back down. I give her a smile tinted with insecurity. This is not going as I had imagined it.

"I…I like to hope that I won't," I answer.

"Hmmm," she says, as she scribbles something in her notebook.

"Are you thinking I'm in denial or something?" I ask her. Damn you, Judy! I'm having some difficulty getting a full satisfying breath.

"No..." she pauses like she was going to say something and then decided against it. She cocks her head and gives me a weird grin. "I think it's great you're not dwelling on death."

This is a support person? Where exactly is the support? Where is the hope? But maybe she's right. Maybe I'm in denial. Maybe I should be getting my affairs in order. And what is she writing in that damn notebook of hers? I should demand to see it, but I don't.

I need to get out of here. I cannot sit in a discussion once a week and feel like this. Not to mention that pregnancy adds a whole different twist to cancer to which I'm sure no one at this place can relate. As our interview comes to a close, I know this will be the last Judy sees of me. Maybe she's rejected *me*, for all I know. Stupid notebook of hers.

My boxing match with cancer is just beginning and I need all the strength I can muster to face down my opponent. I need a coach to rub my shoulders and rasp in my ear that I have the Eye of the Tiger just before I stand up, knock my fists together, and enter the ring.

Plus, after watching that video earlier, I realize the woman in it left me hanging. Did she beat cancer? Is she alive? I don't want to hear anyone else's story, unless there is a happy ending involved. I realize now, too, that hearing about others who are currently worse off than I am only makes me sad and scared. I need something to aspire to, stories that give me hope and maybe even a smile while I trudge through my 'journey.' That is the type of therapy I need. I'm going home right now to hug my family extra hard. And then I'll go on a long walk with my iPod turned way up.

CHAPTER 12

"I Wanna Be Sedated" – The Ramones

I'm keeping my condition under wraps. Outside of my family, I've revealed the whole truth to only a limited number of close friends. For the most part, I consider my situation 'classified,' only sharing the information on a need to know basis. And really, most people do not need to know. It's a lot for others to absorb all at once. I have a hard enough time with some of my friends' reactions — eyes widening, jaws dropping, hand rising to cover gasps, followed by expressions of puzzlement and a familiar litany of questions. It's become predictable and irritating, although I'm sure I'd react the same way if a friend told me she was pregnant with cancer. I am probably being unfair, but explaining my situation over and over is wearing me out. I don't have answers to all the 'what ifs.' I figure the fewer people we tell, the fewer will need updates along the way, which will save me a good deal of work.

Also, I know what I felt when I've heard about others having cancer — pity. And the thought of people feeling sorry for *me* is mortifying. I'd rather push through this and explain things later. I'm hoping that when I eventually tell others of my story it will be in the past tense. I'm aiming for "I remember when I got cancer, and I was pregnant, and about to adopt a baby. Heh, heh. It was so long ago that the details are fuzzy. What a crazy time, though…" scenario. Then I'll adjust my spectacles and turn up my hearing aid.

Out of the few to whom I have divulged my secrets,

my favorite reaction so far has been from my dear friend, Michelle. "Of course you're going to do everything you can to keep the pregnancy and the adoption," she said while she held my hand. "They're your children."

It was just a few days ago, however, that another friend, Deirdre (since downgraded to acquaintance), asked me if we were still planning to go ahead with the adoption. "Really?" she asked in disbelief when I answered yes. "That's crazy. Why would you keep that going?"

"Because I'm completely invested," I began to explain.

"Oh, like financially."

"No! Well, yes, but I don't care about that. I mean emotionally, spiritually…maternally."

"But you haven't even seen the China baby." I frowned. I didn't like that — 'The *China* baby,' like I shouldn't feel maternal about a child from China. Did she mean it like that?

"So what?" I snapped and I could feel my blood getting hot, Mama Bear beginning to emit a low growl from within. "I can't give up. I won't. We all belong together, the five of us. Grant, Ethan, me, and my girls, my *two* girls."

"How do you know they're both girls?" Deirdre asked. Good question.

"I don't. It's just what I feel," I realized as I said it. "And we're connected." Deirdre raised her eyebrows. "Have you heard of the Red Thread?" I asked, knowing she obviously had not.

"Um, no…"

"It's a Chinese legend about how the gods tie a red cord around the ankles of those who are meant to meet one another in a certain situation or help each other in a certain way." All of this was coming out of me and as I spoke the words, I realized this is truly what I believe and that I absolutely can't give up on the adoption. It's destiny. So it looks as though once again, although there is no waiver for me to sign, I am 'refusing to abort.'

I realize I wasn't only explaining myself to Deirdre, but also to myself. By backing me into that corner, she made me fight my way out of it. It felt good to shove her off me and come back at her. Maybe I should actually thank Deirdre for helping me understand my own underlying feelings and, ironically, being the coach I was looking for in Judy. Not that Deirdre understands any of this. She's completely clueless about the reverse psychology she employed. I don't plan to talk to her again for a while.

"But *are* you going to tell the adoption agency?" Jenn asks me one morning while we're on a walk.

"No," I tell her matter-of-factly, "we're not. There's no way they'd let us continue with the adoption and there is no way I'm letting go of it. It's not like they've asked, so we're not *lying* exactly." She grins.

"Right. Good thing, too, because you're a really bad liar."

I smile back at her, "I know, right?"

"Seriously, though," Jenn says, "I don't blame you. It's your family and your business. That little girl is supposed to be here with you…with all of us."

We take a few more steps in silence and then Jenn loops her arm through mine and does an excited skip, "So, you do realize that there is a very real possibility that in the next six months, you will have *three* kids, right? You're going from one to three!" She squeezes my arm as I laugh nervously.

"Crazy, huh?" I shake my head. "Now let's stop talking about it or I think my brain will explode."

❖

Speaking of withholding information, I think it's probably about time to tell Ethan some more about what is going on with our family.

He knows I am having a health issue and that I am working hard on getting better. And of course he is aware of, and very excited about, a forthcoming sister in China, but as for *another* baby, he is completely in the dark. Regarding breast cancer, he has been told, "Mommy will have to get some very strong medicine to make sure the cancer never comes back. This medicine is *so* strong, it's even going to make Mommy's hair fall out." I had said this to him with such a forced insouciance that even *I* started to believe chemo wasn't a big deal.

"You're going to be bald?" he asked me with both disbelief and intrigue. I could tell he was already imagining how that would look.

"Yup," I said, trying really, really hard to form and maintain a smile.

"Will it grow back?"

"It will, but not for a while," I answered, my stomach twisting into a knot.

"Will you wear a wig, or just be bald?"

"I don't know. I'm thinking I'll get a wig, maybe wear ski caps or scarves sometimes."

Scarves? Why did I say that? I don't even wear scarves around my neck because I can't get them to hang right. I seem incapable of making those cute knots or loops shown on the posters at Old Navy, so how could I possibly manipulate one into looking decent on my head?

"Hmm, ski caps are cool," Ethan said, probably imagining all the snowboarding that would naturally be included with this new headgear. "Mom, whatever you do, you'll look pretty."

I looked at Grant who was already shaking his head to let me know that he had nothing to do with Ethan's answers. Either way, my fake smile became sincere in that moment and I hugged him hard. "Thanks, Buddy," I said.

But now it is time to share the rest of the news. I am 18 weeks pregnant and ready to reveal the baby's existence to its big brother. Grant and I sit down with Ethan on the couch for the big talk. He is in the middle of *The Incredibles* for the fifteenth time in the past few months, and is not too keen on pausing it, judging by the 'what the hell?' look on his face, but we insist, as this announcement is sure to be a very big deal.

"So," I begin, as I take his six-year-old hand in mine, "you know how we're going to get your little sister soon from China?"

"Yup," he responds with a single nod of his head, having been in on this plan for as long as we have.

"Well, there's going to be another baby in the family," I say, hardly believing it myself as I hear it aloud. His eyes widen.

"Are we going to *another* country?" he asks excitedly, "to get a brother for me?" Cute.

Grant chuckles and pats Ethan's hair. "No, this baby is in Mommy's belly."

Ethan looks at my stomach, which doesn't look much different yet than it does normally, reasonably flat, mainly because I'm sitting up straight at the moment. He raises his eyebrows and frowns. He's not buying it. Then he shrugs and says, "Okay," and looks back to the paused frame on the TV. He reaches for the remote control.

"Wait," says Grant, stopping him. "Do you have any other questions about this?"

"Hmmm," he says after a slight pause, "is it a boy or a girl? Because I want a little brother."

"We don't know yet," I tell him.

"Well, if it's a girl, then you'll have to get another baby, too, so that the family can be even with two boys and two girls," he concludes.

He smiles at me, grabs a handful of cheddar goldfish crackers from the plastic bowl resting on his lap. I study his face for signs of jest—a smirk maybe? Instead he puts four fish into his mouth and crunches them happily to bits.

Of course there's no smirk. He's six. I take the remote from him, aim it at the TV, and press 'Play.'

CHAPTER 13

"Dance Inside" – The All-American Rejects

I am mere weeks away from heading into the great abyss, also known as chemo. And although I am often convinced that nothing could exist beyond the black wall of fear that is 1/15/08, I need to prepare for the possibility that something might. So off we go to meet my perinatologist, Dr. Holder, for an ultrasound. Dr. Mitchell referred me to him and I was grateful not to have the chore of hunting down another doctor. Admittedly, I haven't even done most of the hunting; Grant has. But I'm sure he's appreciative, too.

A few weeks ago, I opted out of the amniocentesis. Partly, I didn't want to be probed again, especially by a super-sized needle. I also know it can be risky — babies have been lost due to the procedure itself. But mainly, I don't know what I would do with the information if the test were to come back with bad news. After all this time and emotional upheaval, would I be able to handle it if the results showed abnormalities? So instead, I chose to avoid that test, buying myself a few more weeks of ignorance and hence relative sanity.

Today's ultrasound might uncover issues with the baby that could have been caught before with an amniocentesis, but I am choosing not to think that way. Maybe the past few months have made me so insane that I am losing my ability to analyze things correctly. Why don't I feel like making a list of the pros and cons of each screening that's offered? And why don't I have a list of questions with me regarding today's appointment? My situation seems to have pushed me to a point where I have let go of reason and begun to trust more in things like maternal instinct, hope and Grandma June. Rather than coming to the appointment with my notebook and a list of questions, instead I wore my new pink underwear for good luck. And if all goes well today I plan to wear them to every ultrasound.

Dr. Holder enters the room where I am lying on the exam table in my robe, listening to the ultrasound machine whirring softly beside me. Grant is sitting in a chair but gets up to greet Dr. Holder.

"Good morning," the doctor says, "I'm Dr. Holder. How are you feeling this morning, Stephanie?" He has a lovely accent that I, naturally, cannot place, but Grant perks up right away. Ah, he must be Nigerian. Grant mentions that he spent two years in Lagos with his parents when he was a child.

While the two of them bond, the nurse begins squirting gel onto my slightly protruding belly. "It's so warm," I tell her. She grins as she puts it back into what I now realize is a heater on the counter.

"We keep it warm for our patients. It's better, huh?"

I nod. "Much better than the cold stuff. Thanks." Why don't all doctors do this for their pregnant patients? Maybe it's just a perk of being considered 'high risk.' I'll take what I can get.

Dr. Holder moves the transducer around my abdomen, taking many, many measurements of the fetus. I am trying to relax, but it's somewhat difficult. I want to pass this test so badly but I am powerless over the results. It's not like I had a chance to study. My anxiety causes me to begin asking random questions such as, "Does it have a brain?" Like a trained expert like Dr. Holder would need to double check.

"Yes, the baby has a brain…see here?" And he graciously points to it even though it's the biggest part of the whole baby. "It's all there. Everything looks very nice."

"And all four chambers of the heart?" I ask, trying to impress him by drawing upon my next-to-never-utilized anatomy background.

"Yes, yes. All four chambers, and blood flow is good," he assures me, smiling as he continues taking pictures and entering the data. Then he stops what he is doing and looks at me. What? Is it something bad? My heart leaps to my throat.

"Do you want to know the baby's gender?" Dr. Holder asks. I breathe again.

"Yes!" Grant and I say together.

"Please," I add. When I was pregnant with Ethan, we did not find out the gender because Grant and I agreed there are "so few surprises in life" and it would be fun not to know. Not enough surprises in life…well, that was before, when there actually weren't.

Dr. Holder moves the probe around a bit more and then pauses again. "It's a girl."

"I knew it!" I aver proudly. Grant looks at me and raises his eyebrows. "What? I did. And she just passed another test!"

"That's my girl," Grant says as he looks toward the screen at his daughter.

As of now, Dr. Holder has no concerns. I grin, grateful for the power of my pink underwear on the chair, sandwiched between my folded jeans and blouse. "You will return here for an ultrasound after each round of chemotherapy to check for any effects the drugs might have," Dr. Holder informs me with his genial voice.

My stomach clenches at this and I can't help feeling choked by the thought that it will be all my fault if I ruin this perfect baby girl.

As we leave the appointment, I try to focus only on the feelings of hope I came in with this morning, calling upon Grandma June's voice to drown out any negative vibes buzzing about. I'm trying, but it's hard. This 'letting go of control' business is new for me. As they say, Rome wasn't built in a day. But how long *did* it take?

CHAPTER 14

"Livin' On the Edge" – Aerosmith

I need a wig. An exceptionally fantastic wig, that doesn't look at all like a wig. I don't know if anything like that exists, especially in my non-pop star price range, but I'm beginning to research my options. I've sat down at the computer a couple of times and typed in 'beautiful wigs' as key words, but have quickly become overwhelmed by the amount of cancer sites that pop up, and so I end up putting the computer on sleep mode and walking away instead. But it's time to get serious. I'm running out of time if I want to be prepared before chemo begins next week.

I'd like to maintain privacy by ordering something online, having it delivered and waiting for the UPS guy to be driving away in his big brown truck before I open the front door a crack and quickly pull the package inside. However, when I finally make myself commit to more than a few minutes on the internet, I read seemingly endless opinions and scroll through pictures of hundreds of wigs, and realize this is impossible. As a rookie wig buyer, I'm going to have to physically try these things on. There are more decisions to make than I knew regarding color, cut, texture, etc. I think I'd prefer something synthetic because it seems to be cheaper and require less upkeep, but I don't know if it would be 'non-wiggy' enough up close. Considering my unsuccessful internet clothing purchases of the past, I should really just suck it up and go into a store. After all, as one of these online experts says, "A wig is like an outfit you need to wear each day, so make it a good one."

A couple of days later, Mom, Jenn and I pull into the tiny parking lot in the back of BigWigs, a small wig shop in Hollywood. I hope to be headed home from here in about an hour, armed and ready for my impending hair loss.

"Oh no, I'm going to be bald!" I stop in my tracks at the threshold of the shop, stick my arms out and grab the door-jamb on either side of me. My sister gives me a gentle push from behind but I am clinging tightly with my fingers and won't let go. I am paralyzed by the reality of why I am here. Jenn ducks under my arm to get in front of me and turns around. She smiles as she pries my hand off the metal frame.

"C'mon, we're going to find something great."

I follow reluctantly. We wander up and down the aisles, studying the mannequin heads that look back at us with frozen faces. I overhear a woman up at the front telling the cashier that she needs a wig for a play she is in. I am so jealous! How I wish I were here for her dramatic purpose, rather than my own.

"How long should I go?" I ask Jenn, sounding stoic as I try to hold in my emotions.

"Don't go too long," Mom intercedes. "It gets very heavy, and my friend Janet said that she got one that was…"

"I know, I know," I snap. "It was cut like a *pixie*. I don't want to be a friggin' pixie!" An overreaction, I know, but I've heard this story three times already and still couldn't care less. I've never wanted a pixie haircut, despite Mom's frequent suggestions throughout my life that I get one, so why would I want one now? "Sorry, Mom," I add quietly. "But I don't." What I really want, what I've always wanted, is an enhanced version of my hair. Wavier, thicker, shinier. Now where *is* it?

I spot a layered blond to my right and pull it off of the plastic head. I duck behind the curtain of one of the 'dressing rooms' and attempt to put it on. Oh, that is awful. I look completely washed out. I yank it off my head and return it to its rightful owner. In a few minutes, Mom comes over to me carrying two wigs, one blondish, one reddish, both short.

"Thanks," I say as I take them from her hands. I save my eye rolling for when I'm turned away and heading back to the private cell. I try on each one and they are simply horrible—too puffy, too short, and/or dumb-looking bangs.

"Steph? How are they?" Mom is asking through the curtain. I slide the curtain back and hand them to her.

"Nope," I say curtly and walk toward another aisle. My frustration mounts, as does my guilt for my somewhat rude behavior. But I can't help it. This is worse than when I shopped for a bathing suit too soon after I had Ethan. Will I be leaving here empty-handed and eating a bowl of ice cream this time, too? How can these wigs look so good on the mannequins and so bad on me?

After trying on about twenty wigs and being disappointed about fifty times, I am ready to give up. I know that math doesn't add up, but my disappointment is just so huge. Nothing looks right on me. I'm not comfortable in anything, and we've been here for three hours! It is everything I can do not to run out of the store crying and pulling my own hair out, figuring I'll get a head start on the whole thing. Instead I decide to ask a salesperson for help, which I probably should have done when I first entered this stupid store.

His name is Arthur, my dad's middle name, so maybe

he is *supposed* to help me get through this. "What are you looking for in a wig, pretty lady?" he asks me with a perfect cross between a pout and a smile.

"Well," I begin, perking up slightly, "I want *my* hair, only better."

Arthur reaches across the counter and lightly touches my hair. "Honey, I have just the thing for you...it's amazing—I wore it myself in blond for New Year's Eve!"

I smile because Wig Shop Arthur is everything I realize I want in a hair consultant—attentive, complimentary... and fabulous. He turns dramatically on his heel and goes into the stock room, returning shortly with a longish rectangular box under his arm. He removes the lid and pulls out a long (but not too dramatically long), brunette wig. It is shiny (but not too dramatically shiny), and has what looks to be just the right amount of soft curls. He brushes it a little and then instructs me on the correct way to place a wig on one's head, which requires more finesse than flopping it over my hair and tugging down with both hands at once like I'm struggling to put on a turtleneck, which is what I'd been doing. I look in the mirror and both my sister and I exclaim in unison, "That's it!" I look at myself from as many angles as possible with the help of Arthur and his hand mirrors.

"This is the one," I say and finally smile at my reflection. "I'll take two."

We do stop for ice cream on the way home, but it's to celebrate rather than drown my sorrows. Afterward, as Mom and I pull into the driveway, I'm feeling pretty good. I put the wigs on the Styrofoam heads that Arthur had handed to me with a wink, and place them on a shelf in our bedroom closet along with their special hair spray and shampoo, and the nylon head caps to be worn under them. I hadn't known about those either before Arthur's wig training seminar today.

Back out in the living room I notice the answering machine light is blinking. I mosey on over, press play and listen. "Yes, this message is for a Mrs. Hosford. Mrs. Hosford, this is Celina at City of Hope. Please give us a call. We have a problem with your insurance coverage."

Oh no. What? What does she mean a *problem*? Quickly, I grab a pen and scribble down her number and extension. For once, it is not after 5:00 pm on a Friday when I hear this type of message, so I dial her immediately.

"This is Celina," she answers.

"Yes, hi Celina. This is Stephanie Hosford. You called me about a potential issue with my insurance?"

A short pause on her end and then, "Oh yes, give me just a minute..." I hold on the line and can feel my anger starting to simmer. What could be the problem? I'm starting treatment next week already. I can barely process the reality of it, but I do know that I need Dr. Sung at the helm. I'm still clear-minded enough to know that. Celina's back on the line. "Mrs. Hosford? Yes, um, it looks as though we don't take your HMO."

"WHAT?" I yell, instantly going from a simmer to an overflowing, dangerous boil that is about to spill out all over Celina, whom I hate at the moment. "But I thought it was all checked out and cleared," I seethe, jaw clenched.

"No," she replies far too casually, clearly not comprehending the enormity of the wrench that has just been thrown into my plan.

"Well, how expensive is treatment without my insurance?" I ask, having no clue what else to ask.

"Hmm, about $140,000," she has the balls to tell me.

"Fuck!" I yell and imagine Celina's shocked face at my language, which makes me hate her even more. I don't know what to say to her. I don't know how to fight this, to convince this random gatekeeper that she is wrong, that I have to have Dr. Sung and City of Hope.

As I slip down into a dark hole of desperation, all I can squeak out is, "I can't handle this."

"Ma'am?" I hear her ask.

"I can't handle this," I repeat and hang up.

Mom has just come into the room, most likely after hearing me yell "Fuck!" at someone. I am crumpled on the floor crying for a change. "Steph! What happened?" she runs over to me and kneels down.

"I need Grant," I mumble.

"What happened?" she asks again.

"It was City of Hope," I answer, "they say I'm not covered for treatment there. I need Grant."

Mom squeezes my arm. "Oh shit," she says, and I am surprised because Mom rarely curses. Dad always cursed enough for the both of them. "Yes, okay, do you want me to call him?" she asks. But then we hear a key in the front door.

"Grant!" Mom rushes him as he enters. "Call City of Hope right away!" She instructs him. "They just told Steph she's not covered for treatment there."

Grant puts down his workbag and looks at Mom and then at me. "Hold on," he says calmly, his hands lifting up and then pressing down in an 'everybody settle down' gesture. "What is happening?"

I sit up and sniff, "I came home from the wig shop and there was this message on the machine..."

"Oh, did you get a wig?" Grant asks. "I did," I say, recalling my happy, hopeful mood from an hour ago. "But then, the message…Celina says I'm not covered…and it will be $140,000…" I start to whimper again.

"Who's Celina?" Grant asks.

"The woman who *called*," I say, frustrated because I can't get this story out fast enough in order to hand it over. "What are we going to do? I need Dr. Sung. I can't start my search over. She's the one! Don't they understand that?" Grant comes over and sits down next to me.

"Okay, alright," he says and I can tell he's thinking of whom to call first. "Don't worry, bug. I'll handle this part. You focus on yourself and the baby." He takes my face in his hands and looks into my eyes. I know that look. I love that look. Grant is going to fix this. Insurance reps beware.

I'm not exactly sure how he does it, but within a couple of days, a 'special contract' has been drawn up between the City of Hope and our insurance company. My treatment will be covered for a year. Grant mentions something about bypassing customer service reps and schedulers and speaking directly to bosses' bosses.

"The decision makers in any company can do what they want," Grant informs me. "I just made them want to do it."

"Did you make them an offer they couldn't refuse?" I ask him, jokingly.

"Yup," he says. I give him a huge hug.

"Thank you, Don," I say.

"Don? Who's Don?" he asks, totally confused.

"Corleone, from *The Godfather*," I say. Grant laughs and nods.

"Ah, right."

CHAPTER 15

"Stronger" – Kanye West

With my team of doctors in place and my synthetic hair in the closet awaiting the call of duty, I feel somewhat more prepared to take on the challenges ahead. However, I am still having trouble truly imagining what my family is going to look like within the next few months. I need to figure out a way to stay focused and keep my eye on the prize(s).

The Friday before chemo and after my gentle but boring prenatal yoga DVD has come to an end once again, I flip through the channels on TV. I pause on a scene that has a person turning around in a circle with arms spread out and money falling all around her. This is followed by what I interpret as a flashback of the same woman drawing a dollar sign on a piece of paper, holding it up to the sky with her eyes closed. Next there is a forlorn looking man who draws a picture of a heart on paper, holds it up in the same fashion as the woman with the dollar sign, and is suddenly walking hand-in-hand with a brunette on a beautiful beach at sunset. How did all this wealth and true love become reality for these people? I guess I'll never know because I'm not going to purchase the video that is being offered for only $19.99, plus shipping and handling, that contains all the secrets. But I am intrigued by those drawings each actor made.

I am surprised to find myself inspired by an infomercial, but I feel compelled to sketch a picture of my future family. I draw five stick people holding hands in a line from biggest to smallest on a plain white piece of paper. The tallest one is Grant, I am next (with hair), and then Ethan in a base-ball cap, followed by our daughter from China, and at the end stands the smallest figure. We are all smiling. I write underneath us "The Hosfords." I secure it in a simple gold plastic frame and place it next to my bed. My plan is to look at this picture many times every day. I want it to be the first image I see in the morning and the last one I see at night. Who knows? Perhaps there's something to this. And if not, maybe I'll hunt down the creator of that video. Or take a drawing class.

I walk back out to the kitchen for a snack. Stuck to the refrigerator with a small magnet is the invitation to my nephew Jake's first birthday party. Oh, that's tomorrow already. What am I going to wear? I am in that in-between stage, not fitting into my regular clothes but not quite ready for maternity wear either. I feel bloated and my figure gives the impression that I should lay off the beer for a while. I've been unbuttoning my pants for a few weeks now, cover-ing the evidence with sweaters and hoodies, but it could be time to switch to leggings. Aw, but there's Jake, his cute pudgy face looking back at me, beckoning his Aunt Steph to celebrate with him. I smile at him. But seriously, what should I wear?

"I don't want to go," I tell Grant the next day before the event. "I'm too tired," I lie.

It's not only that I can't find an outfit. It's mostly that it's two days from chemo and I'm so scared that I can barely function. I can't think of anything else. All I really feel like doing is sitting at home and reading the list of possible side effects from the drugs a few hundred more times so I can wrap my head around the idea of mouth sores and vomiting.

Not the best way to spend a weekend, but that's where my mind is now.

"No you're not," Grant says, knowing me. "You're just nervous about chemo. But this will be a nice way to distract yourself. And your sister really wants you there. And you know, hon," he continues, "you should really think about writing all of this down, keeping a journal of all you've been through and what you are about to do."

"No way," I shake my head in the negative, "after each day the last thing I want to do is rehash it. I just want to get through it. That's all." I go back to searching through the closet and biting my nails.

An hour later, I'm in the car with Grant and Ethan for the short ride over to Jenn's house. With Jake's gift in hand, we walk up to the door and let ourselves in. I call out my usual "We're here!" and proceed through another entryway into the family room. I slide the door open.

"Surprise!!" What?

I look around the room to see my family and closest friends smiling at me. What is happening? Where am I?

"But...but, these are *my* friends," is all I can think of to say.

My sister comes over to me, puts her arm around my shoulders and says, "I know...this is your baby shower."

I am so overwhelmed with emotion that instead of smiling back at everyone and thanking them for coming, I turn around and run down the hallway and into Jenn's bedroom, still holding the wrapped present from Baby Gap.

"I'm sorry," I sob to my sister after she finds me, following what I hope was an apology to everyone for my behavior. "I just can't believe you did this for me. I hadn't thought about a baby shower at all. I haven't allowed myself to celebrate the possibility that I have two daughters arriving in a few months."

Jenn looks at me straight on and says, "It's not a possibility, Steph. This is all going to happen. And it's going to be great. Crazy, but great. Now let's go." She takes Jake's gift from me and puts it on the bed.

"His birthday really is on Tuesday, you know," I tell her.

"Yes, I know," she says, "but today the party is for you."

I look into the mirror above her dresser, wipe away the last of the smudged mascara, take a deep breath, and walk back down the hallway toward the living room. It turns out that everyone else has known the true nature of this event for a long time—everyone, that is, except for Ethan and Bubbe, who possess similar secret keeping skills.

The whole yard is decorated with a Chinese theme. Paper lanterns hang from the trees and the covered patio. Red tablecloths have been placed on each rented table. There is a Chinese food buffet and party favors are available everywhere in mini takeout boxes. Taped to the windows on the back patio are red posters with gold dragons and gold lettering on them that appropriately spell out 'Double Happiness.' There are also two large calendars put up side-by-side on the garage door, one for each baby girl, covering March through May. Guests can gamble on when they think each will arrive.

There is music. There is laughter, a lot of it from me. And as I look around the party, I realize that these people must truly believe this is all going to work out. I mean, they bought presents and they're putting money on each girl's arrival—not if, but *when*. They can't all be faking it, can they?

"Excuse me," I say to my friend, Susan, as I stand up from the table where we've been chatting and snacking on egg rolls. I head toward the calendars. "I need to place a couple of bets."

There is a long road ahead, fraught with needles and ultrasounds and wigs and maybe even mouth sores. But at the end of that road is another party, a party of five, the Hosford stick figures holding hands. I allow a renewed sense of determination to wash over me. It is time to move ahead with this battle. "Kiss my expanding ass, cancer," I say in my head. "You messed with the wrong mommy!"

Later that evening, as I put my personalized takeout boxes into the fridge, I wonder: Am I a good friend? Before my own crisis, before I really understood how much it means for a friend to show her support, would I have jumped to the call of duty and remained there like many of my friends have? Or would I behave more like a few other friends who have yet even to call me after hearing of my situation. I truly hope I fall into the first category. I think I do, but even so, I make a pledge: If I make it through everything and one of my close friends, or even not so close friends, experiences anything like this, I will be there for her. I will go to her and hold her hand for days, or even just a few minutes, because I know how much it is appreciated. It doesn't matter where she lives or how long it takes to get to her. If she needs me, I will be there. So much about showing support is simply showing up.

I know I should make a second pledge, one that involves forgiving the women who have fallen short in their friendship duties, for whatever reason. But I think I need more time for that one. I'm not feeling it tonight. I want only to bask in the gratitude I feel toward my family and devoted pals, rather than labor over a plan of amnesty for the others. Gandhi said, "Forgiveness is the attribute of the strong," but I'm not up for it right now. My strength is currently being called upon for other things.

THE HOSFORDS

CHAPTER 16

"Pump It" — Black Eyed Peas

Two days after the baby shower I somehow manage to get myself out of bed and into the car in order for Grant to drive us to City of Hope for my first round of chemotherapy. I am absolutely certain I have NEVER been this terrified in my life, and that includes the time I got talked into watching *Hellraiser* when I was in high school.

I am completely silent during the 40-minute drive. Normally I'd be listening to the morning show on KROQ at this hour, laughing at Ralph Garman's "Showbiz Beat." But not today. I'm not sure I've even blinked yet. I just stare ahead at the freeway wishing for more traffic. Why is my chemo appointment on the one morning in L.A. history when there are hardly any cars on the road? We are getting to our destination far too quickly. I'm not ready. No, I am. Let's do this. No! Turn the car around! Let's go back to Maui.

Instead, we arrive at City of Hope's parking lot. It's crowded with cars and my chest tightens. What if we don't find a space? Can we go home then? As I contemplate jumping out of the car and running to *anywhere* else, a space opens up and Grant parks our green Honda CR-V. I could still make a break for it.

We are greeted at the entrance and guided to the check-in line. The woman standing in front of me is wearing a surgical mask and a ski cap. She is so skinny and frail. She looks like a cancer patient. I am not as surprised by this as much as I am horrified. Will that be me soon? Except with an exceptionally large belly? Oh God, what an odd look that will be. Next time I'm in this line someone will probably horrified by *me*.

After we check in, I see the young doctor who works with my oncologist in the hallway and he smiles and waves. I stare at him blankly and continue down the hall toward the elevator in a fear-induced stupor. I hope Grant is responding in a friendlier manner. I still haven't spoken, and when I finally do I say, "I can't do this."

"Yes, you can," Grant says tugging my arm a little so I'll exit the elevator. "It's going to be okay."

My stomach is just beginning to protrude, taking on the appearance of an oversized grapefruit, so I'm already getting more than a few lingering stares when others realize that *I* am the one wearing the white wristband with my name and birth date printed on it in purple, making my way to the oncology department. I wonder what they are thinking.

First comes the blood work. I feel an ever so slight sense of relief when this part is over. One poke down. I have a meeting with Dr. Sung about an hour later. She interprets my blood work as normal, thus giving the final go-ahead to the oncology nurses across the hall. I have the same questions as the last time we met. "Is this really okay? Will it really work?" What I mean is, "Am I a bad mom? Am I going to live?" I still can't decide if I should view myself as the strongest woman in the world or simply irresponsible.

"I am very hopeful. I really do think things will be fine for both you and your baby." *Hopeful*. I wish she had said *certain*.

"Let's go then," I say, "because I can't anticipate this for one more second."

But the Infusion Center is not ready for me yet. I am handed a device that will light up when it's my turn to report for treatment.

"Let's go for a walk," Grant suggests.

We stroll quietly through the building, no destination in mind, but it's better than being still. We pause outside a gift shop where there is an abundance of cancer-related items for purchase — T-shirts, hats, jewelry, magnets, bumper stickers, all with pink ribbons on them to advertise one's awareness of the fight against breast cancer. Last year I would have worn the pink ribbon, exhibiting my support of all those other women affected. But now all that pink is for *me*. I can't do it. It's a prickling reminder of my personal affiliation with this disease and the idea of a pink silicone band on my wrist is disturbing. I am not ready.

Our little device begins vibrating and flashing its lights.

Time to go.

We arrive at the entrance to the Infusion Center and need to be buzzed in through the door. Why all the security? Are people really sneaking into this section? Maybe it's to keep patients in when they freak out and try to escape. It's not at all difficult for me to imagine this attempt.

"You're pregnant," says the nurse, as the doors close behind us. Trapped.

"Yup."

"I've heard of women going through chemo while pregnant, but I've never actually met anyone who did."

"How long have you been working here?"

"15 years."

Great. Gone is my assumption that she is new and that's why she hasn't treated patients like me before. She uses a plump enough vein on the back of my right hand for the IV.

The first medication I receive is an anti-nausea drug. I pray it will help take the edge off my inevitable barf-fest. Grant read that drinking lots of water and being fully hydrated might help fend off nausea, so I have been drinking water constantly. Next, the nurse dons what looks like a hazmat suit.

"What is *that* for?" I ask, getting a flashback to the movie *E.T.*, with me playing the part of the wide-eyed, waddling alien. Actually, I'm not waddling yet but I know it's coming.

"It's to protect me from the toxicity of your first drug. If it touches my skin, I would get burned."

And it's about to travel through my body and there is a baby in there. I close my eyes and shake my head. I should probably stop trying to make sense of all this.

The first drug, Adriamycin, is delivered by what's called a 'push.' It is administered into the IV all at once until the enormous syringe full of reddish-orange liquid is empty. As it begins, I watch in disbelief and barely contained horror as the hideous, syrupy medicine snakes its way through the clear tubing and into my hand to be distributed by my blood throughout my entire being. It feels cold as it enters my hand and I shiver at the reality of it all. A threshold has been crossed. In my head, a door creaks closed behind me. There's no turning back.

"Please, please, please be okay," I whisper, hoping desperately that the baby can hear my plea. I close my eyes and put my hand on my belly. "Put up a force field," I mentally command the placenta and all the powers of the universe. I picture the clear, impenetrable bubble used by Violet in *The Incredibles*. Bullets bounce right off of that thing. I am now thankful I let Ethan watch that movie more times than I can count so that I could summon this image.

Twelve minutes later the syringe is empty, its contents are inside me now and there's nothing I can do about it. A bag full of the second drug, Cytoxan, is hooked up to my IV and hung on the pole. This one is delivered by a 'drip' and is going to take about two hours. "Kill the cancer, leave the baby alone," I silently beg each clear drop as I watch it slide down the tube.

We have with us an insulated bag with food and drinks, and movies to watch on Grant's laptop, as well as magazines, books, crossword puzzles, and a note from Ethan.

"Can I have Ethan's note, please?" Grant pulls it out and hands it to me. I unfold the orange square of construction paper and read "I love you, Mommy," scrawled in green crayon. I hold it to my chest.

Of course I need to go to pee again. Between pregnancy and the water I've been drinking, I need to go every 20 minutes. It is a challenge to drag the IV pole into the lavatory with me and not get tangled within the dangling tubes on my way there, shuffling along in my non-slip socks, or while I'm peeing. Nurses hold the door for my tall, thin, metal rolling companion and me as we enter or exit the bathroom. I look at myself in the mirror as I wash my hands, careful not to wet the tape that secures the IV. I look at my hair, pulled back in a ponytail. Will it really all be gone? What will that be like? What's under there? My hair looks pretty good today, for once. Not its usual puffy self. And I really like the color now, too. I finally found a good one — Cherry Kola. Why must my hair choose now to look so shiny and acceptable to me? Is it pregnancy or the fact that its days are numbered that's boosting its attractiveness? It's like that toy, any toy that Ethan never plays with, is never interested in...until he catches me taking it to the Goodwill bag in the garage. Then it's his favorite toy he simply can't live without. My monthly gray roots don't seem so intolerable after all.

I walk/roll back to our room and there is enough time to watch a movie. I choose *The Jerk* because I need to laugh. It ends just as I'm finally unhooked from the IV. I am free to depart.

Okay, so that's how chemo goes. A segment of The Great Unknown is now known, or at least the administration of it is. But I have the side effects to fear now, which everyone knows are the worst part.

"See you tomorrow?" asks a nurse as we pass by the desk on our way out.

"Oh, God no," I answer immediately. "In three weeks." It then occurs to me that other patients must come in daily or weekly or whatever their particular illness requires. What a horrible thing to endure the very next day.

Knowing I now have extremely toxic drugs flowing through my veins is unsettling, to say the least. "Force field, force field," I continue muttering. I am certain I am a ticking time bomb, ready to explode with nausea and headaches and misery. When will it hit? When I get to the parking lot? Tonight? Tomorrow? I can appreciate a good mystery, but this one sucks.

"I'm hungry," I am surprised to hear myself say as we arrive home. I'm nervous to eat, like each bite I take is going to come exploding back up the second it hits my stomach. I hope that's not how this works, but I really have no idea, so my head is full of dramatic scenarios, and most include voluminous projectile vomiting.

"Great!" says Mom while she's hugging me. "Let's all eat something then."

Dinner is graciously uneventful. Afterward, as I help Ethan into his basketball pajamas, I stroke his hair and tell him, "Thank you for your note, Buddy. I read it over and over today and it helped me feel strong. It made me feel like Wonder Woman," I exaggerate for effect. He smiles wide.

"My note made you a superhero? Cool! You should get some Wonder Woman pj's!" I like that idea.

"Yeah," I tell him, and in my best Samuel L. Jackson voice, add, "Ethan, where is my super-suit?" He giggles.

"Mom, that's Frozone from *The Incredibles*, not Wonder Woman."

"Oh, right," I wink at him.

Maybe if this all works out, I'll treat myself to one of those vintage T-shirts with the 'WW' on it. But right now, it's hard to think past tomorrow.

When I open my eyes in the morning, I lie very still, afraid to move. Slowly, I move my head to one side and wait… okay so far. At a snail's pace I roll the rest of me over to the same side and wait again…still good. Ever so gingerly, I push myself up to a sitting position and hang out for a minute. Nothing happens so I take it a step further and stand up. I'm trying not to wake Grant. He must be exhausted because he rarely sleeps in past 6 a.m. and it's almost 7. I stand by the side of the bed for another minute, waiting. I still feel normal. Cautiously, I venture out of the room, look both ways, as if nausea might run me over, and walk down the hallway to the kitchen. I realize that aside from some slight coughing and a sore hand from the IV, I really do feel fine.

I make it through breakfast, each bite swallowed slowly and suspiciously. But nothing happens. I read my current book and do crossword puzzles all morning. No sneak attacks occur. Should I live on the edge and do my prenatal yoga video? I put it into the DVD player and begin the familiar routine, mouthing the instructor's words along with her. I finish the whole 45-minute long class and I have yet to feel even a hint of nausea or fatigue. What is going on? I know I should be thankful for each minute of calm, but the anticipation is killing me!

Jenn stops over later in the day after work and I describe every detail from yesterday to her.

"And how is it going today?" she asks.

"So far, I'm fine," I admit. "But I know I can go down at any second. Dr. Sung says however I react this time is most likely how it will go every time, so at least I won't have to wonder like this after those next rounds."

"Well, that's good," Jenn says. "But I'm sorry this first time needs to be so mysterious and unknown."

"Seriously," I roll my eyes. "The weird thing is that I feel like I'm actually hungrier than usual. And Dr. Holder told me I should eat whatever I can hold down, even if it's only ice cream."

"Sweet!" Jenn smiles. "I'm happy to join you for your ice cream-only meals."

I go the entire first day without barf. But I have ice cream for dessert anyway, for insurance purposes.

"I was really okay today," I tell Grant and Mom, hoping I'm not jinxing myself by admitting that.

"That's really great, hon," Grant gives me a hug.

The next morning I wake up, look around tentatively, sit up in bed…and feel fine. This is getting eerie. Once again

I carry on as usual, taking Ethan to school and myself for a short walk. I worry that I am getting too cocky leaving the house like this. What if I'm suddenly overcome by side effects on someone's front yard? I walk a little faster toward home. Tomorrow it's all going to hit me hard, I just know it.

The following morning I wake up fully expecting the worst FOR SURE. I perform my usual drawn out, wary getting out of bed routine, tiptoe down the hallway as if I'll awaken the beast if I don't, eat breakfast, and wait. Nothing. But it's the third day! I don't get it. I dig through my file folder and pull out my paperwork with the list of side effects on it. Number 1 — Nausea, Number 2 — Loss of Appetite. I certainly don't want to send them an invitation, but what is the deal?

"I saw the stuff go into the IV," I tell my mom. "I know it's in me."

Does this mean it's not working? I still don't feel sick and I clearly have not lost my appetite — at all. In fact I'm pretty sure I'm eating *more*.

I decide to call Dr. Sung. Two more days have gone by and I am simply doing too well. "Why do I feel fine? What's wrong with me?" I ask her. Did I just utter those questions back-to-back?

But I press on. "Are the drugs not working? Did you give me a lighter dose than normal people?" I think I hear a quiet chuckle at my rapid-fire inquiry.

"No, no. You received the proper amount. It's based on a patient's weight, remember, and I did not hold back because you're pregnant. It's the placenta shielding the baby, not a lesser volume of drugs," she explains. "And not feeling sick has nothing to do with whether they're working or not," she assures me. "You may just be lucky, or it could be that the baby is actually helping you to tolerate things because your body is working to protect both of you."

"Does that mean the baby is absorbing it all instead of me?" I panic, but then remember she just told me the baby is protected, so that probably sounded dumb. I'm so thrown off by this unexpected stroke of good fortune that I can't think straight.

"No, not at all," she responds patiently, adding, "you should probably just accept this as a good thing. Call me if anything changes."

"Okay," I answer, trying to ignore the guilt poking at me for tolerating chemo so well while others suffer so horribly.

"Don't feel guilty," Grant tells me later, "you finally lucked out with something here. Embrace it."

"You're right," I agree. "I'll try."

But as it is against my nature to simply accept things, I assure myself that my next round in three weeks will get me, no question.

In between chemo appointments, it is imperative that I stay healthy. If I get sick, it could throw off my whole treatment schedule. I'm working with a deadline here, trying to be done with these first four rounds a few weeks before my due date, so I need to take germ warfare seriously.

I've stocked up on hand soap and sanitizer and have been trying my best to resist the temptation to touch my face, which is proving difficult. I never noticed until now what a constant corner of my eye toucher, ear rubber, and nose scratcher I am. If I got a dollar every time I went to touch some part of my face, I'd be able to finance Ethan's first year of college within a day, or maybe a week, if he goes out of state. "All this sanitizing is kinda stressful," I tell Grant as I whip a mini Germ-X out of my purse and slather my hands with it in the Trader Joe's parking lot.

"Well, whatever works," he says as he finishes unloading the grocery bags from the cart. He closes the trunk.

"Here, I'll take the cart back," I say, grabbing it and starting to wheel it quickly toward the entrance.

"Steph..."

Shoot. At least I didn't zip up my purse yet.

CHAPTER 17

"Makes Me Wonder" – Maroon 5

A week after my first chemotherapy experience, we receive a call. It's the adoption agency to inform us we've been matched up with a baby girl from China. Oh my God, oh my God, oh my God! I do a hoppy little jig and my eyes well up. This is finally going to happen! For a moment I forget all that has transpired in the past few months and imagine boarding a plane to China to bring our daughter home. I will be the first of our family to hold our long-awaited bundle. I can almost feel the weight of her in my arms.

"You'll be getting the paperwork in a couple of weeks, which will include her picture and some basic information about her," says the woman on the phone.

"This is so exciting!" I exclaim, smiling from ear to ear.

"And you'll need to fill out and send back the travel documents for you and your husband. You'll probably leave in mid-March," she informs me. That seems like forever away, but we've waited this long, so what's a couple more months? I'll need to distract myself somehow. Hmmm, what's the weather like in China in March?

I feel a tap on my shoulder. Annoyed, I brush it off. But then I feel it again. Jeez, *what*? It's Reality. And it's shaking its head and wagging its finger. I look down at the floor. Oh, right…that.

What am I thinking? I can't go to *China*. Sweat forms on my forehead and in my armpits. It's getting hotter in here by the second. Oh crap, I'm nervous. Thanks, Reality. I've rehearsed this in my head several times, what I would tell them when they call with an update, but now I'm forgetting everything. I got lost in my excitement. I start to remember what a horrible liar I am and feel my throat constrict. The next few minutes and how this woman responds to what I am about to say are pivotal regarding the outcome of our adoption. Thankfully this person can't see me right now because I doubt she'd rush to hand over a child to the pale, sweaty loon I just caught a glimpse of in the mirror.

Relax. I take a deep breath in an effort to pull it together before I open my mouth.

"Well, I'm actually not going to be travelling," I reveal, praying I sound confident and unaware of any problems this might cause.

"Oh? Why not?"

"Well..." I pause. Grant and I have already made up our minds not to tell my whole story, but telling part of it truthfully is enough for me to feel justified in holding back the rest of it. "I...I'm pregnant, actually." I close my eyes and wait an eternal two seconds for her response.

"Congratulations!" She sounds sincere. "Well, your husband can travel, right?" she inquires. I exhale and nearly drop the phone in relief.

"Oh, yes. Absolutely. Grant will be travelling, probably with his mom." I try to play it off a bit more, but not so much that she gets suspicious. Of course, why would she ever assume that there's more to this story? This isn't an episode of *Law and Order*. I assume she's not a detective searching for any nuance of incongruity. But I tack on, "You know how these things go. Heh-heh. Just when you least expect it..."

"It's not the first time I've heard of this happening," she says.

I'll bet the rest of it would be.

"And you know you'll have to do the re-adopt paperwork right away when they come home," she instructs, "to make everything official and give her U.S. citizenship."

"Oh, of course, we will do that immediately," I respond. I have no clue what this entails, nor do I care. I'll do whatever it takes when the time comes, once my daughter is here with me. I will research how to go about the re-adopt process the second I hang up this phone. She'll be more official than the Presidential Seal.

"We need to decide on a name," I say to Grant after replaying what I now consider to be my Oscar-worthy phone performance for him. He is duly impressed.

"I'm proud of you, hon," he says. "That must have been uncomfortable for you not to admit to everything."

"I was definitely sweaty and shaky at the time," I say, "but I just kept thinking of that family portrait I drew, and in the back of my head I was thinking, 'This is *our* family, and we know what is best for our family, so stay out of the way.'"

"Nice," Grant nods his head, "and that is totally true, so you should feel nothing but good about that."

I smile. "Okay, so back to her name." We have discussed this at length on several occasions and have gotten as far as knowing we want her name to begin with 'N' for my dad. This narrows it down considerably, especially since Norma and Nanette were voted out immediately. I like Nikita, but as she probably won't grow up to be a French assassin, it doesn't really fit. Nanna brings to mind an old white woman and Nessie makes me think of a sea monster. I find Nicki cute, but Grant associates it with a woman who annoyed him at some point. So really, it's among Nicole, Natalie and Naomi. "Nicole is too close to Nicki," Grant points out.

"Okay, and I don't want her nickname to be Nat," I add, imagining a gnat. "I love the name Naomi. I think it would be adorable on our little Asian daughter when she is young, and beautiful when she is an adult."

Grant pauses a moment, I can tell he is picturing this. "Agreed. Naomi it is," he decides.

"Yay!" I say. "And I want her middle name to be June," knowing I will not negotiate on this. But Grant's smile tells me there will be no need.

Twelve days later, we receive a large envelope. The return address is that of the adoption agency and it's all I can do not to fling the rest of the pointless mail onto the floor and run into the bedroom to tear open the envelope by myself. But I resist, and instead wait impatiently for Grant to come home so we can do this together. The second he walks through the door, Ethan, Mom and I rush him.

"It's here!" I squeal, waving the precious parcel in his face.

"Dad! It's the stuff about my sister in China! We're waiting for you to open it. Come on! Let's go!" Ethan is tugging on Grant's hand.

"Okay, buddy," Grant says, putting down his bag. He's smiling big. "You've had the envelope for two hours and didn't open it? Impressive," he says toward me.

"I know," I agree. "It was tough. But we should all share

this moment." We all walk into the den and stand facing each other in a tight circle. "Shall we?" I ask.

"Open it, Mom!!" Ethan is jumping up and down. I stick my finger under the corner of the sealed end, rip across the folded seam and then reach my hand inside to pull out the thin packet. The first page is a congratulatory letter. Very nice. But I take that off and put it on the bottom.

And there she is, Xiang Yi Guan, soon to be Naomi, her serious little face looking back at us. I let out a small gasp.

She is propped up against a plastic indoor slide and wearing far too much clothing for being indoors. "And I love her," I proclaim without a second thought. That's it. A love connection has been made. All set from my end, anyway. Another picture is a close-up of her face. Wow, she is gorgeous. Her shaved little head (most likely to avoid lice in the orphanage) does nothing to detract from this fact. I hope I will be so lucky with my own shaved head, but I'm not starting out nearly this cute.

I caress her photo paper cheek with my thumb while Grant reads through some of the other pages. According to her reported birthday she is 16 months old now. There is some sparse health information about her in the packet and tidbits like "enjoys blocks" and "prefers lights off to sleep." She is currently in an orphanage in the industrial city of Guangzhou, which is in the Guangdong province in southern China. But she is already a part of our family. I know it. I feel it as I gaze at her face and gently touch its image. Her solemn expression speaks volumes. I bet her first 16 months have not been easy, but she is clearly a survivor. "Just like your mom," I say to her picture. "We are going to help each other get to a better place, you and me." I imagine the red thread tightening around my ankle, our kinship strengthening. "Your dad is coming for you soon."

But then I start to sniffle when I see the portion of the packet with the travel information. I am heartsick that I will not be joining Grant on this very special trip. We had planned for years to go together, take Ethan with us and maybe even travel for a few days in Beijing before joining others in our adoption group. I can barely stand the thought of not being the first one in our family to hold Naomi. But this is how it has to be, the new reality.

"Don't worry," Grant says, looking at my watery eyes and protruding lower lip. "We'll *all* go back to China one day. I promise."

CHAPTER 18

"Big Girls Don't Cry (Personal)" – Fergie

It's happening. My hair is falling out.

It's right on schedule, 19 days following chemo, and everything I'd heard it would be, and by that I mean that it sucks. The process began a few days ago when my scalp started aching and my hair felt heavy, like a toddler was tugging on fistfuls of it and refusing to let go. Then, in the shower, I witnessed the first round of casualties, small bundles of wet hair dropping from my head, swirling around the drain. The next day the bundles were bigger, making audible splats as they landed on the floor of the tub. When I made the mistake of then brushing my hair, loads of it ended up staying in the brush, a wet and tangled brunette mass. It's depressing.

I know I can't stop the exodus, but I've been attempting to deter it by simply not washing or brushing my hair for the past four days. I'm not sure how far I thought this would get me, but it seems like dreadlocks could possibly form and now my scalp is seriously in pain from the tugging weight of my hair plus the excess grime that has collected there. I need to do *something*.

Okay, fine, you stupid hair! Who needs your split ends anyway? I step into the shower sans cap and perform what I believe will be my hair's final wash. Clumps upon wet clumps crash down as I fruitlessly shampoo and condition the doomed mop. Damn, this really is happening. That's a lot of hair by my feet. I turn the water off, gather the collection with my hands, step out and throw it into the bathroom trashcan. I dry off, pull on the clothes I had on before the shower, and attempt to put a comb through my hair. That's when it happens…the chunk that falls off and leaves a bald spot. Fairly large and on the front left section of my head. There will be no hiding this. My eyes widen and I gasp at my reflection. Jesus, it's super-white.

"Oh God…yuck," I say aloud, leaning toward the mirror and grimacing.

Unfortunately, no one is home but me, which might be a flaw in my plan. What was I thinking, doing this alone?

My breathing becomes shallow. This is it. I am going to bed tonight as a bald woman. I start crying. What should I do right now? I can't keep brushing it and watching it fall onto the counter and into the sink, dying a slow, ugly death. And I certainly don't need to wake up each morning to tufts of it on my pillow followed by a game of Count the Bald Spots. Where's the dignity in that, for God's sake? No, this has to happen quickly and in one sitting.

I don't want to disturb Grant at work for this, but I need someone to be here immediately if not sooner, before I lose my nerve. I frantically call my sister.

"It's time!" I cry into the phone.

"What do you mean?" she says, sounding scared and confused. "Are you in early labor?"

"No, it's my hair," I sob, "my hair is falling out in huge clumps and leaving bald spots…it's time to shave it off, but no one's here."

"I'll be right over," she says, "with Bobby's clippers."

"Okay," I squeak, and then sit on the floor of the bathroom so I don't have to look in the mirror at my mangy head.

The accounts I read on the internet about women who shave their hair off once it starts to fall out seemed so inspiring at the time. They must have left out the part where they wept on their bathroom floors, rocking back and forth chanting, "It's only hair, it's only hair," while knowing it's so much more than that.

Jenn arrives to find me in a crumpled heap with my hand covering my newly exposed scalp. I'm embarrassed to show the ugly spot even to her. Just as she had to pry my hand from the doorjamb in the wig shop, my sister now needs to unglue it from my head. She helps me to my feet and we both look in the mirror at my reflection. I frown.

"Well," Jenn asks, "shall we go for it?" I look at the patch where the circle of skin the color of a cotton ball is glaring back at me. There's only one way to make the bald spot go away, short of using a Sharpie.

"Let's do it. Shave it all. I want this over with. We need to put this hair out of its and my misery."

Just as Jenn plugs my brother-in-law's clippers into the socket, we hear Mom come home with Ethan from his after school program and Grant come home early from work. They all enter the house at the same time.

"We're in the bathroom," I shout. "Come say goodbye to my hair!" I try to sound brave for Ethan, hoping he can't hear the quiver in my voice. They all come down the hallway and enter the room. It's getting crowded in here, but at least it's my favorite people.

"I'm just guessing now, but I think the first step is to make a ponytail and then cut it right the hell off just in front of the elastic band," I suggest. I interpret everyone's shrugs as agreement and twist an elastic band into my hair, like I do just about every day. I suppose this will be the last hair accessory I'll need for a while. I ask Ethan to do the honors and with Grant's help, he snips off the majority of my shoulder length locks.

"Oh thanks, Buddy," I say sincerely, "my head feels so much lighter." I smile at him, but then look at the severed tress in Grant's hand. "Please throw that away...outside," I request. "And there's some more in the trash can here that can join it."

"Do you want to take a break?" Grant asks me when he comes back into the bathroom.

"No. Just do it."

The shaving begins. The buzzing sound of the clippers is deafening, like a fighter jet is flying too close overhead. But this is the only way I can think of to take control of my situation, or at least the hair loss portion of my situation.

Grant and Jenn alternately take turns while Ethan and Mom look on. I do a portion of the shaving myself and feel a sense of recklessness as I move the clippers from the front of my head to the back. I am finally the rebel I was always too mainstream to be.

"You have a nicely shaped head," Grant says when it's done, the clippers silenced at last. We all look in the mirror at my exposed dome.

"Thanks, Honey," I sigh. I feel both strong and queasy at the same time, but mostly queasy.

Jenn is wrapping up the electrical cord and Mom is smiling at me in the mirror. Is she forcing herself to hold it together for me as I am for Ethan? Ethan rubs his hand over my scalp, which thankfully has not revealed any Gorbachev birthmark islands on it, at least.

"Feels cool, Mom." I smile as best I can, but my eyes are watering. I excuse myself and go into the bedroom. I don't

want Ethan to see how sad I am quickly becoming about
this. There's no Kleenex box in the room, so I use my shirtsleeve to dab at my eyes. I take a few deep breaths to pull
myself together and notice my shirt not only has a heavy
sprinkling of hair on it, but also a small dribble of something else on the front. Vanilla yogurt, maybe? I take off
the shirt to change it, pausing to look at myself in the full-
length mirror.

"Yup, there it is," I say to my new reflection, a large per-
centage of which appears smooth and round. "The look every
woman wants." I slide my hands over my head again back
and forth. Any feelings of defiance have dwindled, probably
the shortest streak in the history of streaks of rebellion. I am
spent from the whole ordeal and want only to crawl into bed
and hide under the covers, but resign myself to stay awake
and dry-eyed for Ethan until he goes to sleep.

I have neither felt nor appeared sick thus far, but looking
at my head, it's nearly impossible not to associate myself
with cancer. Seeing a bald woman usually indicates she
has a life-threatening disease, doesn't it? Of course, under
normal circumstances she'd also be skinny, so at least I
don't fit that part of the stereotype. Or do I look that much
more pitiable? I miss my hair.

I am supposed to see Dr. Mitchell tomorrow morning,
but it seems far too soon to enter the public realm in my
newly hairless state. Can't I have a day to mourn my loss
and get used to this new shaven identity? On the other
hand, I don't think I will ever be used to it, so I should
probably just go.

The next morning is visually painful as I am greeted by
my pinheaded reflection in the mirrored closet, reminded of

yesterday's events. I feel the baby kick inside me, like she's telling me to stop grieving and get moving.

"Alright, little girl, I hear you. I'm going," I speak to her, taking comfort in our communication. I get ready for my appointment, leaving plenty of time for wig placement and adjustment. It really doesn't take very long though, thanks to Arthur's instructions.

I leave the house feeling vulnerable, like one false move and my secret will be revealed—I'm not the pleasant-looking pregnant woman with nice hair, but actually a bald lady in the midst of a battle against an evil villain. And possibly on the verge of madness.

"I like the new hair," Dr. Mitchell compliments me as he walks into the exam room where I'm waiting, reclined on the table.

"Thank you," I respond, touching one of my new curls. I put on makeup today, which has never been an everyday ritual for me (having nothing to do with being 'natural' and everything to do with laziness), but it is in fact helping my emotional state, so I should really consider putting in the effort more often.

I am happy to learn that everything seems to be going well with the baby, but not excited that I need to schedule a glucose test to make sure I'm not developing gestational diabetes. I knew this was coming and have been dreading the required blood test for weeks already. I'd hoped to become more cavalier about needles by now, but no. I should probably accept that our relationship will never improve. Dr. Mitchell tells me I need to get the test done within three weeks. I plan to call the lab from home and schedule it for exactly 21 days from now, no sooner.

The following day I need to venture out again because it is time for the second round of chemo. I'm not scared into a catatonic trance like before the first one three weeks ago, but I am still nervous and my head, as smooth and tangle-free as it is, is bringing me down. I lack the motivation to put on makeup or my wig even though I was committed to these acts just yesterday.

"No hair today, hon?" Grant asks as I go past him out the front door wearing a blue ski cap.

"What?" I snap back, irritated. "You don't want to be seen with me like this?" Grant frowns and shakes his head.

"No, honey, that's not it at all. I just thought that you like your wig and you might want to show it to Dr. Sung."

"Well, I'm not feeling it today, so you'll both just have to deal with that!" What is wrong with me?

My lip quivers and Grant reaches for me, pulling me to him as my mournful tears start to fall.

"You do whatever you want, hon. You always look beautiful to me. I just want you to feel good."

How does he do that? How is he consistently so much nicer to me than I am to him? I know I should feel nothing but lucky about that. But instead, I feel even more irritated. It's been building up for a while I think, and I know as soon as I open my mouth I'll regret it, so I should just…

"Why are you so nice?" I blurt out.

"What do you mean?"

"I *mean*, why don't you ever cry with me? I don't understand how you never break down. I've seen you well up during *Hoosiers*, but never about this."

"You want me to cry? Is that what you want?"

"Yes...no...I don't know. But it's always me. Only me. You and Mom and Jenn, you're never anything but positive. Aren't you scared? Any of you?" A long pause. Oh no, now I've done it.

"Steph, I don't know what you want. You think I always know how to be around you? Well, I don't. But why would I possibly think that crying in front of you would help you out?"

"I...I don't know." I look down at the ground. The fact is I don't know what I want from him, or anybody. I just want this all to be over. I want to be on the other side looking back.

"The truth is when you were first diagnosed I was scared, really scared of losing you. And yes, I had my moments, but I kept them private." When he says this I want to take it all back, but it's too late, obviously. Why did I do this to us?

It's the first time I'm hearing these words, but I've essentially forced him to admit them to me, and I don't know whether that was fair.

Maybe he needs to keep his emotions to himself. Maybe it helps him maintain his focus. Maybe I'm just a nut job who doesn't know when to keep her mouth shut. I've made Grant go to a place he probably doesn't want to go, which was selfish. And the truth us, I *don't* want Grant to cry with me. I need his steady calm to keep me afloat.

"But now it's different," Grant continues. "Now we know what we're up against for the most part. You're Stage I. The cancer hasn't gone anywhere. Yeah, the treatment will suck for you, but we can handle this."

Phew, he's back.

How could I think those closest to me are unaffected by my situation? They are all sensitive, caring, realistic people.

It's not that they haven't shed tears. They just haven't let me see them. I comprehend now that it must be a conscious effort on their part. But I can't ask them about it because it *could* actually make them cry with me, and I just now realized that I don't want that. And neither do they.

As we make our way down the hallway at City of Hope, up the elevator and down another hallway toward the Infusion Center, I notice others staring at me a bit longer than the last time I was here. They appear as uncomfortable as I do as their gazes go from ski cap to belly and back again. I suppose I could have worn something other than maternity clothes to hide my true state, but I don't know that a trench coat would make me any less noticeable. I guess I should get used to being stared at around here. But hey, perhaps I am actually helping other patients feel better about their own situations. Maybe they are comforted to know that while they might have cancer, well, at least they are not me.

We begin with the requisite blood draw during which I attempt to improve my own mood with a small joke by referring to the phlebotomist as "Stabby Joe." He doesn't seem to see the humor in this, in that he doesn't laugh at all. Did I just offend a man with a needle in his hand? His name *is* Joe, but from the looks of him he was probably a toddler during the *Friends* era and so does not understand the allusion. I'll stick with this reasoning rather than assume he doesn't find me funny.

I attempt some more small talk, but Stabby is not receptive. *Come on, Joe. I'm not having a great morning so can't you humor me with a wee chuckle?* I smile at him, hoping

I'm conveying that last thought telepathically. He removes the needle, puts the cotton ball on my arm, wraps Coban around it and sends me back out to the waiting area, all without a word. I hope he doesn't remember me next time.

When I get in to see Dr. Sung, she disagrees with my choice to wear the ski cap. "Do you like your wig?" she asks me. I shrug.

"I actually do," I admit to her, "it's kind of glamorous, really." I go on to recount how Arthur introduced Wig and me to each other.

"I love that story," Dr. Sung smiles. "I'd like to see the wig on your head next time. If you like it, you should wear it. If something makes you feel good about yourself, don't save it."

I'm still allowed to feel pretty? I think I held back on my cosmetic efforts this morning because aside from my general moodiness due to today's impending infusion and the many months of baldness ahead, I subconsciously assumed that beauty and cancer don't go together, that I somehow have no right to feel attractive. But that could possibly be my most flawed theory to date. Now is the time I need to feel the *best*. Starting tomorrow I shall recommit myself to Wig. And maybe even get a new lip gloss.

My blood work results come back fine and I am given clearance for chemo. Once again I imagine a force field around my daughter as I watch the toxic drugs enter my body. I try my best to relax. Grant and I watch movies. I order and eat lots of food from the menu in my room. The infusion goes smoothly again but I am more than eager to get the hell out of there. At last, I am unhooked from the IV.

The days that follow are just as magnanimously uneventful as the time before. Again, I dodge the barf bullet and am therefore able to keep eating as usual. I continue to justify my food indulgences by telling myself I should store up in case nausea decides to suddenly spring itself on me with a vengeance. But I'm fairly confident now that it won't happen.

A week passes and it is time for another ultrasound with Dr. Holder, the perinatologist. I am especially anxious for this one. I have a lot of drugs flowing through my system now and this test will let us know if it is affecting the baby's development and/or growth. There is nothing I can really do to prepare, but last night I at least made sure my lucky pink underwear was clean and in first place position in the drawer for today.

Dr. Holder moves the transducer all around my belly. I gaze at the screen hoping to recognize something on it. I wish I were better at interpreting ultrasound images. I never know what I'm looking at, even after being told. "Oh, right, I see it now, sure," I'll say as the doctor or tech points things out, and I'm squinting and tilting my head sideways, hoping the figure will become obvious, like in those cool 3D stereogram images where the subject pops out if you just relax and let yourself go cross-eyed. I'm not good at those either.

Dr. Holder is taking a whole lot of measurements again, and I'm thankful when he finally begins to translate the quantitative data into words. "The spine looks great," he tells us. I breathe a little easier.

"What about the brain and heart?" I ask, going for some more of the basics. He points at a small black and white silhouette that even *I* can see is beating rapidly yet rhythmically.

"The heart looks wonderful. It really is fine so far." He glides the probe slightly and presses in. "Her brain looks good, too," he assures me, pointing out each beautiful hemisphere. "Everything is where it should be and the blood flow looks normal."

I smile, but I want more, more indicators that she is okay. "How about the liver, spleen, stomach, intestines, and the um...okay, everything. How is EVERYTHING??"

Dr. Holder looks me in the eyes, smiles and says in a most comforting voice, "Don't you worry. Everything is fine. She's going to be great."

I look past his friendly, bespectacled face toward the machine with the representation of my daughter still squirming away on it. I think of Naomi, across the ocean in China. Each daughter is in her own world, unaware of our connections, of how much they are each wanted and awaited. "Just hold on, girls," I say inwardly. I am speaking to all three of us.

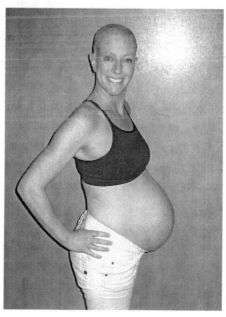

I'm smiling? I must be crazy!

CHAPTER 19

"Move Along" – The All-American Rejects

I think I found our new home. I didn't mean for this to happen now, but I did have that fleeting thought a few months ago that adding distractions to my life might be a good idea, so maybe that was interpreted by the universe as a request. We've had no formal discussion on the subject, but now that I think about it, Grant is probably under the logical assumption that our home search is on hold, as it *would* seem rather ludicrous to continue looking while dealing with everything else. So then why have I been secretly stalking a particular house for the past few months? This is a question for my future psychotherapist.

It is only a mile up the hill from my mom. It's been very easy to cruise by once a week or so to see if the 'For Sale' sign is still posted on the front lawn. I've tried to play it cool with the listing agent, like I could take the house or leave it, but being that I've toured the home four times, he might be on to me. It was initially listed far out of our price range, and way too expensive for what it is—a simple house, not big, not especially modern, not surrounded by more valuable real estate. But there is something very tranquil about it that speaks to me. I saw a family of deer trotting across the street during one of my first few drive-bys and I was hooked. Part of me wants it to be sold to someone else already so I can move on and put it out of my mind. However, my latest inquiry of the realtor who was holding yet another open house has left me somewhat excited because the asking price has begun to drop.

I know I should just let it go, but instead I bring Grant up to see it.

"Isn't it great? Isn't it excellent for us?" Grant tours around rather silently taking in each room. I'm sure he's noticed that it even has a blue bedroom for Ethan and a yellow one for the girls and a bedroom/bathroom for his parents when they visit from Washington.

"Yup, it's pretty great," Grant admits. "It's still too high for us though." I stick out my lower lip and sigh.

"I know. And I know it's ridiculous to consider adding this to our situation right now…"

"Tell you what," he says, looking out the window in the small kitchen onto a beautiful view of Los Angeles. "If it drops again, which it probably won't, but if it does, we can talk about insulting them with an offer."

"Deal!" I agree, hoping I have not seen the view from this kitchen for the last time.

I'm not sure if fate is smiling upon or laughing at us, but within a week the asking price drops again.

"Okay, let's give it a shot," Grant tells me after I share the news. Of course, by dropping the price, other hopeful families are making offers, too, damn them. But we put forth our best offer, plus a note mentioning that we have no home to sell, that we are ready with a preapproved loan, and that we really love this house.

"Should I have mentioned our current 'situation'?" I ask Grant, putting up finger quotes around 'situation.'

"No," he says, "it's too much…and they might not even believe it anyway because it sounds so preposterous."

"Good point."

For the next three days, I try to busy myself with some prenatal yoga and shopping at Target for Grant's upcoming China/Naomi trip. It's a very long list of items, so I am distracted from thinking about the house, although yes, I am thinking about it a lot. I'm assuming we will be outbid because it has happened more than once in the past with other houses, so when our agent calls us on the third day, I am not expecting her to exclaim, "You got it! They accepted your offer!" But that is exactly what she says.

"Oh Jeez. Really?"

Are these good heart palpitations I'm feeling? I think so! And thus begins the mad flurry of paperwork and negotiations that ensues when a home transfers ownership.

"Are you out of your mind?" my friend Maggie asks when I tell her we are about to buy a house. We have been chatting on the phone and I find myself slightly annoyed by her response. Again I think back to my pre-cancer self and wonder if that would have been me last year. Would I have inserted my unsolicited opinion rather than respect a friend's decisions and simply support her? I hope not. At least I know I would never do that now.

"I don't know anymore, maybe," I answer, suppressing the urge to hang up. "You know, you can't always predict when things will happen in life."

"Yes," she retorts, "but you don't have to buy a house. This isn't happening to you, you are making it happen." Yes, I am! And why should I have to justify this? I swallow hard so I that I don't blurt out "Shut up! I have my reasons!"

Do I need to explain the hope for our future the house is giving me? That this physical structure symbolizes my new faith in myself, that it's giving me confidence that I can fill the empty rooms with my children? That I feel inner peace when I stand in the backyard and look out over the trees to the mountains or see those graceful deer on the hill a few feet away? For Christ's sake, hasn't she ever heard of *nesting*?

"Right," I respond instead, and then after a pause, "Well, I must go pick up Ethan at school now. I'll talk to you soon." Neither of those statements is true.

While I'm busy battling my inner second-guesser, wondering if Maggie is right and I *am* out of my mind to buy a house right now, the date for my glucose test sneaks up on me. I would so much rather be choosing a new paint color for my living room that is not yet in escrow than at a lab ingesting the super-sweet concoction I've been given. I chug the whole bottle within the required minute and then wait exactly one hour before alerting the staff that I need my blood drawn. Following that nuisance, I go home, feeling quite relieved, and check the test off my mental to-do list. The next morning, however, that check is mentally erased as I learn from Dr. Mitchell that I failed the test. Damn it.

"What does this mean for me?" I ask him on the phone.

"Well, in a few days, I'd like you to go back to the lab and retake the test, but this time your blood will be drawn four times."

"*Four times?*" I try not to yell.

"Sorry, but yes. And bring good reading material because it takes a few hours."

Oh, I am so over all this sitting around and getting stabbed by needles.

But three days later, I am back in the lab gulping the

sweet drink and having my blood taken every hour. In a constant state of anxious anticipation, I alternate between watching the clock and trying to focus on the book I brought with me. How in the world will my veins survive this assault? After the fourth and final prod, I roll down my sleeve, stand up (pausing to make sure I don't keel over), and head home. God, I hope I pass this time.

I come home to a message from our real estate agent, Nancy. We are officially in escrow.

"Now we can really start to negotiate things," Nancy says.

"Great!" I reply, although I am already worn out by the thought of it. I just want to move in. I am also a week away from chemo #3. The stress stemming from the house is mostly good and exciting, but stress nonetheless.

Conversely, there is *nothing* good about the stress regarding my next round of chemo. If I truly concentrate, I can sometimes get to a place in my head where I can convince myself that I should be thankful for cancer treatment, that it is at least good I exist in a day and age and country where I have this option. I can hold these positive thoughts for a good three minutes, occasionally four if I remember to appreciate that I haven't needed to shave my armpits, legs or bikini line for a while. But then dread seeps through the cracks in my wall of positivity and quickly floods my brain. There is no getting around the fact that chemo sucks, no matter how 'lucky' I am to be able to receive it.

CHAPTER 20

"Fighter" – Christina Aguilera

As I strive to stay afloat, immersing myself in activities such as setting up our home loan, meeting with our agent for a house inspection, and picking out Valentine's Day cards with Ethan for his class, we get a phone call from the adoption agency. Grant will be travelling to China in about three weeks. He will be away for two weeks once he gets there. I look at the calendar. Shoot. This means he'll be gone for my fourth chemo round. It's hard to imagine Grant not being with me for that.

"Okay, great. I'll let him know," I tell the agency woman. After hanging up with her, I immediately pick the phone back up and dial Jenn's number.

I need to ask her if she can come with me to Chemo #4. I feel a little guilty because I know she will accept my invitation despite her job, her two young children and being newly pregnant herself. But has there ever existed a family without some sacrifice and some guilt in the mix?

I have a new ream of paperwork to complete in a short amount of time. This will allow Grant to carry out the adoption abroad without my being there. During the next couple of weeks I will be driving all over Los Angeles to different government buildings with another file folder. This file folder, the Adoption File, is hard-sided, has a handle on the top and a lock on the front—a far more sleek and sophisticated look than the cheap one I slapped together for my health records. It houses all of the myriad documents, reports and applications (all with official stamps, signatures, etc.) that I have kept track of for two and a half years. I've worked hard to keep everything up-to-date. We are so close to having the Naomi piece of the Hosford Puzzle in place. There is no way I can slow down now.

China frowns upon the adoptive mother being pregnant while adopting, so much so that they could opt to halt our process. I get it. The adopted child should receive as much undivided attention as possible. I can appreciate that rule. But I simply can't follow it. Naomi will get all the love and attention she deserves, I am sure of it. Thankfully, our agency here in the U.S. sees it this way, too, and has thus advised us to write a Letter of Explanation that should contain a viable reason (other than pregnancy) why I have 'chosen' not to accompany Grant to pick up Naomi. In other words, I need to lie.

I've bent the truth before. I might have inflated the number on Ethan's kindergarten reading log by a few minutes so he could attend the in-class ice cream social, or perhaps I told Grant I got 1240 on the GRE when really it was more like 1180. Harmless. But deceive a foreign government? This will be a first.

Motherhood is a most powerful phenomenon in that it provides us with an instinct to do whatever it takes to be with our children. Still, thank God this will be a written work and not something I need to say in person. I hem and haw about what I should write. If only I could tell them that

I'm not *choosing* to stay behind, that it is actually tearing me up inside that I cannot travel to China and be the first in our family to hold my daughter, that I'm really not the type of mother who places anything ahead of her children. But I'm stuck. I need to come up with something else.

I type up a short and rather vague paragraph explaining that my grandmother is very sick and I must take care of her, that to leave her now would be irresponsible of me. I tell Bubbe about the letter and apologize for saying she's ill. She couldn't care less.

The letter, along with some other documents, must be notarized. This is not a big deal. I have had so many things notarized during the adoption process that the guy working at Mailboxes, Etc. whips out the notary logbook for my signature and the inkpad for my thumb when he sees me pull into the parking lot. Next, I need to take the notarized paperwork to a place downtown to be authenticated because I guess the notary cannot be fully trusted. I don't know. This part is new for me.

Three days after dropping the documents off, I return to the same office building to pick up them up and take them to the Chinese consulate. "But what if they question me?" I ask Mom. "What if they notice I'm pregnant and pull me into the back room and I crack and reveal the whole truth?"

"That won't happen," Mom assures me as we leave for the consulate. "But maybe you should wear some really loose clothing."

I wish Grant could do all this or at least accompany me, but he is on a business trip in New York and it needs to get done immediately or he won't be able to join the group going to China this time. I know this is most likely our only shot at getting Naomi. Adoptions to the U.S. have slowed down so much in China lately that if we miss out this time, we could be set back for years and who knows if we'd ever be allowed back in line. And even if we were, it wouldn't be Naomi, and that is simply unacceptable.

I'm already sweating as Mom and I pull up to the consulate building. Just act natural, I tell myself as we go through the front double doors. I take a deep breath and a number. It's kind of like the DMV in here — a hot mess of people speaking in many languages going from one walk-up window to the next hoping to have their paperwork accepted. Mom and I sit down in two of the numerous uncomfortable, hard plastic chairs and wait our turn. We try to pick seats as far from others (and their germs) as possible. This place is probably not high on the list of recommended venues when going through chemo, but what can I do? I am tapping my foot nervously and putting my shirtsleeve over my mouth and nostrils when my number is called. I make a concentrated effort to walk rather than waddle up to the window. I smile, hand the clerk the papers and hold my breath. She looks at them and then back at me, asks for my ID, looks at it and then me again.

"Okay, thank you…next, number 62 please."

"Am I done?" I ask her. She is already looking past me and to the person holding number 62 behind me.

"Yes," she says curtly, clearly moving on.

"Oh, okay," I mutter. I look over at Mom and motion for her to join me. She stands up and walks over.

"What's wrong?" she whispers.

"Nothing, I think. Let's go."

I take her arm and we are out the door before anyone can say, "Lying, pregnant white woman."

❖

In the middle of this paper chase, I reported to City of Hope for chemo round #3. Having gone through the glucose-testing marathon just days before, I was surprised I didn't bleed air when they attempted to draw my blood.

There was no mistaking that I was pregnant at the appointment. Everywhere I went I felt like I was in an old Western movie entering the saloon through the swinging wooden doors while everyone goes silent and just stares, waiting to see what the outsider reckons she'll do. I wasn't as bothered by their ogling as I was curious—did they think I was insane? Unaware of my pregnant status? On the wrong floor?

"I'm like a unicorn," I told Dr. Sung. "I see people gape at me as though they've heard of such myths as pregnant women receiving cancer treatment, but assumed they were only the stuff of legend. They look at me and then whisper to each other."

"Yes, well, you are part of a very small group," she said matter-of-factly. I frowned. Whenever I imagined being part of a small, exclusive club, this was not what I had in mind. What I envisioned had included a yacht or maybe an unusually high IQ. I realize my lack of either has thus far delayed invitations to join such alliances, but my 'Cancer Plus' membership is by no means a substitute. I just hope I *never* have to renew.

CHAPTER 21

"Lose Yourself" – Eminem

Grant is leaving for China. My mother-in-law, Shelby, is going with him. I am insanely jealous. It is supposed to be me on that plane, and there is absolutely nothing I can do about it but try my hardest to concentrate on the magnificent fact that in 14 days they will return with Naomi.

My feelings for this little 17-month-old girl who is living in an orphanage on the other side of the world are so powerful. I can't explain the connection I feel when I look at her picture, but I know she is my daughter and that is all I need to know.

"Just go and get her," I tell Grant as I hug him tightly on the curb in front of the airport terminal.

"I will, Bug," he assures me. And then off he goes with a suitcase full of documents, powdered formula, antibiotics, pink onesies and the power of attorney to sign his name on whatever might need my signature over there.

The weeks when Grant will be gone are filled with appointments, so at least I'll be busy.

It is time again for Dr. Holder and another ultrasound. For this one, Mom comes along. This is her first time accompanying me to one of these and it hasn't even crossed my mind how emotional it might be for her. I have been getting into somewhat of a groove with my weekly screenings, tests, infusions, etc., and have become far calmer than I was a few months ago. At this point, I feel fairly sure that sometime in the near future I am going to be the mother of three. It's taken me awhile to get here but with Grant halfway around the globe picking up one very real little girl and an image of another very real baby on the screen to my left, it's difficult not to believe.

For Mom, though, I think reality is hitting hard because she is being uncharacteristically silent.

"I can't believe it," she finally whispers, looking at the ultrasound, "there she is." She takes my hand. "I'm so proud of you," she tells me through some tears, squeezing me tighter.

"Thanks, Mom," I sniffle. Dr. Holder informs us the baby is doing very well.

"Things are looking just as they should for both of you," he says.

"I have just one more round to go, you know," I tell him.

"Yes, I know," he says, nodding his head, "and I will see you after that one to make sure all is well."

"We're close, aren't we," I put forth for confirmation, "to actually pulling this off?"

"It's just around the corner," he smiles. Mom's grip on my hand becomes a vise.

The next day I have a meeting with realtor Nancy in order to continue negotiations on our potential new home. I can't wait to be done referring to it as 'potential.' While Grant has power of attorney in China so he can sign paperwork for me, he has given me power of attorney here in the U.S.

so I can sign real estate documents for him. So it actually *is* possible to be two places at once.

On my end in the U.S., this is a bit scary though, being that of the two of us, I am not the one considered the dealmaker.

I don't haggle well and tend to get too emotionally involved during these sorts of exchanges, even if it's bargaining over an overpriced toe ring in Venice Beach. And there might have been one particular occasion when Grant requested that I "wait outside" the dealership while he handled a car purchase. I really want this house, so I am going to have to keep myself somewhat together, despite my predisposition at this moment to be even more impatient than usual.

With Nancy's help, I am able to finagle a new roof, some electrical updating and a bit of chimney repair. I'm rather proud of myself as I hold my ground for these things, although truth be told if the seller hadn't agreed to them, I probably would have caved and continued with the purchase anyway. But I don't have to tell Grant that part.

Breaking news from Guangzhou: Naomi was brought to Grant yesterday, handed over by her caretaker in the orphanage. Through the magic of e-mail and a blog Grant set up before leaving the U.S., I have been able to keep tabs on his journey. Tears drop as I read about the tiny toddler being placed in Grant's arms, how she stares at him with quiet curiosity and confusion, but soon snuggles onto his shoulder. My own arms ache with anticipation to experience Naomi's physical presence.

Grant writes that she can walk but is fairly wobbly, hair is on her head again but dull and broken, and her skin is a little sallow. She has but two teeth and she weighs 17 pounds. *17 pounds?* I think Ethan weighed that at six-months-old.

Naomi also has an awful cough, but Grant has already mixed up an antibiotic elixir from our pediatrician to give her. Poor little lungs. Grant says that the air quality is so dismal in Guangzhou that he's considering getting them all surgical masks to wear on their excursions. "Who would have thought you'd ever miss the air in Los Angeles so much?" I type back to him.

He also says Naomi is tough and feisty, having no issues pushing her miniscule self into a large group of older children, grabbing a toy from the biggest one and walking casually away with it, confident there will be no retribution. I can already tell this daughter of ours is going to teach me a few things about survival.

Grant in China wearing Naomi and a diaper bag

My preoccupation with the house and with the Naomi updates has sped up the arrival date for my fourth round of chemo. Jenn and I make our way up to the third floor to check me in for the day. I am fairly huge now at 32 weeks and am ever aware of the stares from the other patients and visitors as I sway through the hallways. Thanks to pregnancy and the liters of water I've been drinking I need to pee now every six minutes.

"I should really just tell them to set me up in the bathroom," I tell Jenn, half-joking.

Somewhere in between restroom visits I get my blood drawn, meet with Dr. Sung, and get connected to an IV.

"Let's finish this," I say directly toward my protruding belly. "Force field up." Jenn smiles and puts her hand on my stomach.

"Last one, my little niece," she whispers. "Hold on tight."

During the four-hour-long infusion, Jenn and I watch *The Princess Bride*, which happens to be my favorite movie of all time. I've watched it countless times. It contains everything it claims it will: "Fencing. Fighting. Torture. Revenge. Giants. Monsters. Chases. Escapes. True love. Miracles." Today it seems extra appropriate for me to watch this movie, as I feel like I've experienced half of those things over the last six months in my real life. But the main thing is that it makes me laugh—a lot.

We eat, we catch up on gossip, read the tabloids, make fun of the celebrities, and vow that the next time we do these things, I will not be attached to an IV pole, but rather we will both be receiving spa pedicures.

When I am finally unhooked, we head down the hallway and out to the car. If I weren't so huge, I'd be running to the parking lot, but instead I'm held back by this slow, laborious waddle. I try not to think about the fact that I am *not* actually done with chemo. I have to return here for four more sessions a few weeks after what I hope and pray will be successful childbirth. I desperately want to enjoy a sense of freedom, but it is really difficult, knowing that the road ahead is still so long.

But now if I'm ever in a game of 'I Never' and someone says, "I've never gotten chemo while I was pregnant," I'm pretty sure I'll be the only participant who will be able to drink to that one. So there's that.

CHAPTER 22

"Father and Daughter" – Paul Simon

Following a two week stay in one hotel room, standing in line after line to complete paperwork in various governmental offices by day and trying to soothe a screaming toddler by night, my husband and mother-in-law have boarded the plane to come home.

It is Friday, March 21, 2008. I know that because Jenn is holding a poster she made with "Welcome Home Naomi" and the date scrawled on it in pink glitter. It's beautiful. We hold balloons and stuffed animals and as we wait huddled together, I can hardly stand the anticipation. Two and half years and a dozen hurdles and we are finally here. I've pictured this moment a million times. Up until a few months ago, in my mind I'd been in the group deplaning, of course, walking up the ramp to be greeted by my excited family. Instead, though, I've been listening to Ethan during the last hour and a half ask, "When will they be here?" every five seconds while he races all over the smooth floor of the terminal in his shoes with wheels in the heels, narrowly escaping collisions with innocent bystanders.

Bradley Terminal is busy this evening, and we are in the main pickup spot for passengers arriving on international flights. I am wearing my wig, makeup, and my favorite maternity outfit for the occasion because I don't want to scare her or anyone else here by not putting in that effort. Los Angeles International Airport is probably another venue not recommended as a place for me to spend time if I want to avoid germs, but there is no way I am staying home tonight.

I'm nearly jumping out of my skin as we continuously scan the groups of passengers who exit through the double doors searching for Grant, Shelby, and Naomi among them. When it's an Asian group, we are especially focused. Finally, the doors open once more and within this group we notice a few Caucasian couples either carrying or strolling with Asian children. This is very encouraging. We line up at the railing, where I need to shove a few people aside in order to get the best view when they don't respond to my "Excuse me." Gentle shoves, of course, that I can always blame on my girth.

A few moments later, there they are. Two very tired-looking adults with the most precious and adorable bundle I have seen yet. I begin waving frantically.

"Woo-hoo! Hi, Honey!" I shout to Grant and we all run, with me pulling up the rear, to the place where they will exit the ramp.

"Oh my God," I croak, anxiously reaching for the little girl I can't believe is actually here.

"Hi, Naomi, I'm your Mommy," I tell her as I hold her for the first time. She stares at me blankly, most likely wondering who the hell I am, what I am saying to her, and why she is now straddling a large, clothed beach ball, but she doesn't scream or cry or try to escape from me, and that's all I can hope for at this moment.

After being strapped into a car seat for the first time in her life, Naomi is silent the whole 40-minute trip home from the airport, gazing out the window at the night sky and the cars whizzing by on the freeway. Sometimes she looks curiously over at this woman who is sitting next to her in the back seat and holding her hand maybe a little too tightly. I can only imagine how odd and overwhelming this experience is for her. She has just spent two weeks in a hotel room with people she doesn't know. She sat (or didn't sit, but mostly toddled endlessly up and down the aisles, according to Grant) through a very long airplane flight, which eventually arrived in a foreign land where she was greeted by a group of overly enthusiastic and smiley strangers speaking a language that is still very new to her. To befuddle her even further, we are now getting off the freeway and into the very definition of suburbia, which can be scary for anyone.

We all unload out of our cars and into Mom's house. Naomi is greeted by a huge, wet lick on the face by Rio the Loveable Lab to which she thankfully reacts with a smile. She is then offered some Cheerios and fruit, while we all stare at her, smiling and clapping madly after each bite she takes.

By the time Jenn and Bobby leave, it is very late and we put Naomi to bed. She goes to sleep in Ethan's former crib that has his old sheets on the mattress. The sheets are still cute with their multi-colored zoo animals and tiny stars, but I feel a twinge of disappointment knowing that had Naomi arrived a year earlier, the crib would have been decked out with brand-new stuff, just for her. However, timing and circumstance have bumped new baby bedding sets to the near bottom of my list of priorities.

When I was pregnant with Ethan, I viewed each nursery item as crucial to his infant surroundings, from what outlet cover would coordinate with his lamp to making sure the pillow on my 'glider' chair was copacetic with the border on the walls. Tonight I'm not sure where the receiving blankets *are*, much less if they match anything.

I know these superfluous details of nursery décor are ultimately unimportant, however, on some level I long for the ability to concern myself with them. It would mean my life was not being dominated by far more stressful factors.

Naomi falls asleep every night fairly quickly on her second-hand sheets. However, her internal clock has been turned completely upside down, so she also wakes up each night around 2 a.m. for the first week. As much as I want to stroll around the block in the middle of the night with a rambunctious toddler, I am simply too pregnant to do this, or at least that's the excuse I give as Grant groggily heads for Naomi's room again. "Sorry, hon," I whisper to him, struggling to at least turn over. But by the time I say this, he is already gone.

A lot of our time is spent at home, which is actually Mom's house because we are still in escrow with our new place. I would love to be more active with Naomi, but I am so huge at this point that venturing beyond the front door takes a good deal of effort. Considering all the recent changes in her world, Naomi is handling her adjustment to us and to her new surroundings quite well. At least, I think so. What do I know really? It's not like she and I are having deep discussions about her emotional status. All I know is she giggles a lot, eats a lot, rests on my belly comfortably and seems to really enjoy playing with her brother and dog.

I love Naomi so quickly and so fiercely that it's almost frightening to me. When I hold her in my arms and we look into each other's eyes, I know we have been connected long before Grant brought her home to us. And I would do it all over again, break any rule, risk the wrath of any government agency, to get to Naomi. She has yet to speak her first word, either in Cantonese or English, but we laugh together more each day and there are countless hugs and kisses and lots of clumsy dancing around the house together to my never-ending playlists...the happy ones, of course, not the angry, swearing, I hate cancer ones.

Today, however, we shall emerge from the homestead and out into the great wide open of Pasadena.

"Do you want me to come with you?" Mom asks.

"No thanks. I want to her to bond with me out there, rely only on me for comfort. I read that's good for our relationship actually," I say, blaming my adoption book.

"Oh, okay," Mom says, dejectedly. I'm thrilled Mom and Naomi are thick as thieves already, laughing all the time, going for long strolls together, but today will be just the two of us.

"Next time, for sure," I promise with a pang of guilt. I hug her after strapping Naomi into her car seat.

The plan is to pay a visit to Target followed by an appointment for a blood test. Shockingly, this appointment is not for me. It is for Naomi. It has been recommended by her pediatrician as a way to make sure she has received the vaccinations that the authorities in China claim to have given her. I hate the thought of a needle in her teeny arm and fear that I will lose some of her trust I have been trying so hard to gain. But I also don't want her to have a bunch of unnecessary shots if she doesn't need them. I really hope our stop for ice cream on the way home will reestablish my fun mom status.

I am aware that Naomi and I stand out together in public.

I've known we would since my honeymoon when Grant and I decided to adopt a child from Asia. During our previous outings to run minor errands, people have definitely given us lingering glances that neither surprise nor bother me, especially since many people offer up friendly smiles with their review. I imagine the chances of blending into the crowd have been reduced even further, now that I'm sporting a giant pregnant belly while pushing a stroller. But as I wait in line with Naomi to purchase our various and sundry items from Target, I feel as though the cashier, who happens to be Asian, is about to burn a hole through my forehead with her glare. She fixes her gaze on Naomi who is sitting in the cart swinging her little legs and holding tightly to my sweater sleeve. This woman has more than what I would call innocent curiosity. It's more like she's demanding an explanation.

I decide to look directly at her and smile as I finish unloading my items onto the conveyor belt. She does not smile back, which annoys me, but is nothing compared to what I feel when she comes out brusquely with, "Her father is Asian?" as she motions her head toward Naomi.

"No," I reply simply, deciding in that instant to refer only to Grant as her father. The woman then cocks her head, looks at my belly.

"So you just like Asians then?"

What? What does she mean by that? Is she thinking I had an affair with an Asian man? Is she thinking Naomi is some sort of collectible? Should I/we be insulted? But here in the moment, I merely hand her my credit card.

"Um, I guess so," I mumble and accompany that with a weak smile. That's it? That's all I have? I sign the receipt. Totally lame.

I have *got* to come up with some better material for when these situations arise, I realize as I push my cart toward the exit.

I'm sure to come up with some zingers in the car.

That experience is followed by our visit to the lab where Naomi's blood draw is even worse than I have anticipated. They poke her arm twice and get nothing. She screams as I hold her on my lap. I try to keep her still while stroking her hair and whispering soothing phrases in her ear.

"You're okay, baby," I say softly. "Mommy's here." But I am totally ineffectual, as she begins shrieking even louder. The phlebotomist then grabs for Naomi's other tiny arm and I beg out loud for him to find a viable vein.

"I'm sorry," he says, and I do feel for him. Mercifully, the blood begins to fill the vial. It takes what seems like an hour to get three tubes semi-full before the needle is finally extracted and I waddle out of there as fast as I can holding her in one arm and pushing the empty stroller with the other. That makes two of us now with an aversion to needles.

Ice cream is no longer an option on our way home, but a necessity. I am so happy to see a messy chocolate smile form on Naomi's face as she dives enthusiastically into the cone overflowing with sugary goodness. I hold it for her and realize that she might love chocolate ice cream even more than I do, and that is saying something. Of course, weighing in at 17 pounds, she can afford a few more scoops, unlike her not 17 pound mom.

Despite our crazy day, we end it in my favorite fashion. I sit in a big comfy chair with Naomi resting on my oversized stomach, her head on my shoulder, while I read to her from the collections of Sandra Boynton and Todd Parr. Sometimes the baby kicks and punches wildly inside my belly when Naomi's tiny body is draped over me. Those moments are almost surreal. I like to think she is bonding with both her future sibling and me at the same time. Ideally, we would have more time as a family of four before the next expansion, but it simply isn't meant to be. Each day that goes by is another day closer to the arrival of her and Ethan's baby sister. We are so close.

CHAPTER 23

"Hey Mama" – Black Eyed Peas

By now my visits with Dr. Mitchell are occurring on a weekly basis. I am back in the stirrups, this time with a fetal monitoring device next to me, its sensors stuck to my belly.

This baby is being charted more than a hurricane off the coast of Florida, but I'm not complaining. The peeks into her amniotic world help me to keep focused out here. On my own in the exam room, my only job is to push a button with my thumb when I feel the baby kick. I'm not convinced I should have been left alone with this type of machinery. I continually second-guess myself as to whether I'm feeling an actual kick or imagining it, overthinking what should be an easy assignment. A strip of paper with two almost parallel ink lines of continuous peaks and valleys steadily exits the machine. Oh no, did I just miss a kick while looking at that paper? Should I push the button now just in case? Is it too late? How about now? Oh, was that another one while I was wavering about the existence of the one before it?

"Sorry if the results don't make sense," I warn Dr. Mitchell as he enters the room.

"I'm sure you did well enough to give me a general idea," he smiles, reaching for the printout. He slides his hands along it, interpreting the markings.

"You and the baby are doing really well," he says, nodding his head. "I doubt we will need to deliver by C-section."

"Really? That's great!" I reply and try to maintain focus on the shorter recovery time that comes with a vaginal delivery rather than an impending episiotomy.

"I do think we should induce you though," Dr. Mitchell adds, "because it will give us more control over your situation. We don't need any more surprises in your life at the moment."

Amen.

We go into his office to look at the calendar for May. I've always been fond of the number 18, but this month the 18th falls on a Sunday.

"Do you do Sundays?" I ask Dr. Mitchell, completely serious. He smiles.

"I mean do you *schedule* Sundays?" I imagine in his profession he's received surprise calls to deliver babies for every hour of the week.

"Yes, I do Sundays," he says.

"Then May 18th it is, please," I declare.

"Sounds like a good day to deliver the peanut," he says, jotting down my request.

Peanut. Adorable. But it reminds me that this peanut needs a name. Grant and I need to get serious about this. We've thrown a few possibilities around, but nothing has stuck.

I work to push myself up and out of the chair. "Okay, see you on the 18th then at Huntington Memorial Hospital," he confirms, escorting me out. "Unless you go into labor before that, of course."

"Oh, right," I say and smile, although the idea of losing the shred of control I have just gained is not welcome. This also reminds me, though, that I have no idea where exactly I am supposed to go on my delivery day. I've only been to that huge hospital once and it wasn't to Labor and Delivery.

I am usually so much more prepared for things. I only

have two kids now. How will it be with three? I begin to understand how my friends with multiple children can leave the house wearing mismatched socks — not their kids, my *friends,* and not just white and off-white, but white and *blue.* What if this is only the beginning of my brain turning to mush? Between chemo and pregnancy, there is so much potential for memory loss. I wonder if I'll still be trusted to operate the toaster.

"Okay, hon, we have two things to accomplish in a short amount of time," I inform Grant that evening.

"Does one of them include moving into our house?" he asks. "Because we just closed escrow."

How could I forget this? We closed escrow today. It would probably help to actually read my day planner now and then after scribbling things into it.

"Um, okay three things," I tell him.

"What are the other two?" he questions. "One is to name this baby," I say, pointing up my index finger. "And two is to schedule a tour of Huntington." I put up the second finger.

"Oh, and we are inducing labor on May 18th," I add. See? Two can play the Toss Out a Major Life Event to Your Spouse and Act Casual About It game. Though I suspect I'm the only one playing.

"The 18th?" Grant asks. "That's in ten days." Right.

I feel my stomach begin to clench at the thought of everything to do. So much for casual.

"Okay, you recruit a few friends to help out with the move. I'll call about a hospital tour and getting our stuff out of storage. And let's name this peanut now!"

At one point, some months ago, I had considered naming her after my oncologist, the only woman on my team of doctors, but then morbidly decided against it because in the back of my head I thought, "What if Dr. Sung's treatment plan doesn't actually work, and I die from this anyway?" I doubted Grant would want that constant reminder. Dark, I know. I think I'm in a better place now. At least a good portion of the time.

As I'm brushing my teeth it hits me. The perfect name for my daughter has presented itself. Did Grandma June just pay another visit to help me with this? I look around me suspiciously, as if she'll appear and say, "You're welcome."

"How about Samantha Reese?" I shout to Grant excitedly from the bathroom with a mouth full of toothpaste.

"What?" he asks. "You want to name her Samfa Wee?" I nearly choke as I laugh and spit in the sink.

"Samantha," I say with a minty grin, entering the bedroom. "Samantha Reese." I look at him with eager anticipation.

"Samantha Reese," he repeats pensively, which is already encouraging because my suggestions up to this point have been followed by an immediate and emphatic "Nope" or we quickly spiral downward into tired absurdity like, "How about naming her Batgirl?" I give Grant some time to ponder while I construct the nightly wall of pregnancy sleeping pillows between us on the bed. Nothing says love like dividing the bed into two almost equal sides, my side being bigger.

Another minute ticks by and Grant finally responds. "I like it."

"Yay!" I clap and then seize the moment, making my way over to the computer to do some quick research to make sure we're not committing to a name that has a negative origin. I can't exactly give my kid a name that means 'Unabomber' in Gaelic or something.

As it turns out, Samantha means "listener." It's an excellent fit. Her progress in utero indicates she has been listening when I've told her to put up her force field for each of my treatments. Additionally, my internet investigation uncovers that people with this name "fight being restricted by rules and conventions." Now I know this is true for sure. She's been fighting both of these since the day she was conceived. Plus, 'Sam' sounds like a cute and tough little girl and I have no doubt that she will be both. Samantha and I have one more ultrasound in five days to check on her.

"We're almost there, Sammy," I assure her before I nod off. "I love you."

Sammy. I smile at how it rolls off my tongue.

The next morning, I figure I should probably pack a bag with a few things for the hospital as I guess I could go into labor before the 18th. At least I don't have to pack shampoo or a hairbrush. But what clothes should I bring? I know I'll be stuck in a hospital gown for part of my visit. How many others before me have worn that thing? I crinkle my nose. I intend to spend as little time as possible in one during my stay. If I recall Ethan's delivery, then something with an elastic waistband will be appreciated, along with an over-sized shirt. This time I have no illusions about fitting into anything less forgiving. I also need to choose an outfit for the baby and maybe get some of those Newborn diapers that pull on my heartstrings whenever I see them because they are so unbelievably small. Naomi is a big help, pulling items out of my overnight bag as soon as I put them in.

Next, I call the hospital to schedule a tour. There is one this Sunday and we are added to the list.

"Okay," I say to Naomi. "Let's go pack up the rest of our stuff into boxes for our big move to our new house." I touch my fingertip to her dainty nose.

She cocks her head, takes my hand and leads me to the moving boxes we purchased the other day. Man, she's learning English fast. I'm glad one of us has a fully functioning brain.

Mom helps me transfer our clothing into suitcases and fold up our bedding.

"You don't have to take everything, you know," she says, rolling up Ethan's Power Rangers poster. I put my arm around her.

"How about I leave my skinny clothes here? I won't need those anytime soon." I'm not kidding. Mom smiles but I can tell she's feeling a wave of nostalgia.

"We couldn't have done any of this without you, Mom," I tell her, and she knows I'm referring to both affording the new house and handling these past nine months.

"And we are moving out in the nick of time," I joke to lighten the mood. "Three Hosfords invading your home was one thing, but five? That's too much to ask of anyone." I nudge her hip lightly with my own. "Plus, a grown man should be able to dash naked from his bedroom to the bathroom without fear of bumping into his mother-in-law, don't you think?" She nudges me back.

"Oh, I suppose so."

"I'll only be up the road a piece," I squeeze my arm around her tighter, surveying the luggage and open boxes around the room. "Oh, I meant to leave these here," I say, reaching for our bathing suits that have been placed into a fabric tote. "I'm sure Ethan and Grant will be here all the time to swim this summer."

"Not you?" Mom asks. I picture myself bobbing around in her pool, hairless and postpartum. I shiver at the image.

"Mom, do you really want your neighbors turning you in for harboring a manatee at your private residence?" We both laugh, but then she shakes her finger at me.

"Don't you call my daughter a manatee. She is a beautiful, strong, wonderful mother."

I grin and revel in this feeling of self-sufficiency. There is something exceptionally gratifying about a parenting compliment from one's own mother.

I hire a moving company to handle retrieving the bulk of our stuff from our rented storage unit in Pasadena. Then I reserve a small U-Haul for Grant to move our things from Mom's house. Aside from these tasks, I can safely say I am of next to zero assistance on move-in day, as technically I am not supposed to be lifting anything or exerting myself. However, I do manage to call out many instructions to the movers and Grant and the friends he has enlisted to help out throughout the day from the comforts of the sofa while I sip Crystal Light, rummaging through a few of our boxes and wondering why in the world I packed up a bunch of pens, pencils and dirty rubber bands a year and half ago and placed them in storage. Was I thinking there would be a shortage by the time I got them out?

After cutting the professional movers a check and sending them on their way, I make another key phone call to order pizzas for Grant and his friends.

"Thank you, everyone," I say, holding up my Hansen's

Diet Tangerine Lime Soda to toast them. They are all drinking cold beer and it looks uncommonly good.

The first night in our new house is peaceful. Both Naomi and Ethan sleep soundly in their own rooms, she in her crib and he in his bunk bed. Grant and I camp out in the guest room on our old bed as our new one is in transit from Pottery Barn. It was ridiculously expensive, but I am able to justify it to myself by looking at it as a housewarming/make-up anniversary from last October/Naomi and Samantha welcoming gift to ourselves.

The next morning, Grant and I arrive at Huntington Memorial Hospital and once we have been shown where to park and what elevator to take to the Labor and Delivery unit, I am ready for the tour to end. "Ten more minutes," Grant requests, but I am nervous and tired and have no patience right now to listen to the neophytes in our group make arguments against epidurals before they've felt even the slightest first twinge of labor. Some of these women aren't even due until the fall. Even I didn't need *that* much prep my first time.

We are ushered into the auditorium to watch delivery videos and receive pamphlets. There are a few plates of cookies set out so I decide we can stay for a bit longer. Along with the snacking, I also preregister for my hospital stay, now only six days away. As I hand in my paperwork, the nurse looks at my 'Date of Intended Admission' and her eyes grow wide.

"Wow," she remarks. "I'll put yours on top."

We are home for all of ten minutes when Grant announces that it is time for a family photo. "What? No way!" I tell him, assuming he's joking. "In case you haven't noticed, I am a huge bald whale. There is no way anyone is going to take my picture like this. Like I'd pay someone money to immortalize this!"

"First, you are not a whale," he responds, as a good husband should. "Second, we are not hiring a random photographer. I'm talking about just us and setting up our own camera on the dining room table."

"Oh," I say, only marginally more open to the idea.

"I really think we should capture this moment because soon you won't be pregnant anymore, and your hair will grow back."

"And what a splendid day that will be!" I aver, but then concede. "Oh all right, I guess we need proof of this whole insanity…but let me at least put a little mascara on the few eyelashes I have left."

My request is granted and we thus proceed to take a few pictures of me in all my smooth-headed, big-bellied glory. Some of these involve me standing solo, a few are with Ethan, Naomi, Grant, or some combination thereof. My two basic poses consist of either standing sideways in order to enlist the belly's profile or standing while facing the camera. We also take some photos with my wig, but mostly without because who besides our family will ever see these anyway?

After the photo shoot winds down, I scroll through the images on the camera. "Oho, look out Victoria's Secret models," I shake my head and have to laugh, "you're all just lucky I'm not the least bit capable of wearing stilettos right now or you'd all be looking for new jobs."

CHAPTER 24

"Closer to Fine" — Indigo Girls &
"I'm A Believer" — Smash Mouth

As hard as I've tried, I'm unable to stay angry with my body. Having felt initially betrayed because it formed cancer so deceitfully, I've slowly regained a sense of respect for it. A small stockpile of admiration has accrued. How can I continue holding a grudge against something that has protected my daughter from harm for so long? Still, the final ultrasound appointment today will let me know if my body will remain in my good graces.

In the stirrups yet again in Dr. Holder's exam room, the machine quietly hums next to me. I look at the black screen lit slightly at the top by the glowing green LED letters that spell out my name (last name, then first, followed by my middle initial, as always) and the date. Will I truly be meeting Samantha in less than a week? I want so much to believe that what my doctors have been telling me this whole time is the truth—that my toxic wasteland of a body has not affected this unborn baby, that the drugs coursing through my veins for the past four months have taken their toll only on me and not her. Please not her.

Dr. Holder enters the room, the nurse close behind him. "Good morning," he says, with his customary friendly smile.

"Good morning," Grant and I respond together.

"So this is our last meeting, eh? Your baby will be born Sunday?" he asks while the nurse retrieves the gel from its warmer.

"I believe so," I answer. "We've decided to name her Samantha."

"Very nice," he says. "Alright, let's have a look at Samantha." Dr. Holder squeezes the gel onto the transducer probe. I let go of Grant's hand to slide the bottom of the cotton gown up enough to allow Dr. Holder to place the probe on my prominent belly. I feel its gentle pressure, the gel warm and smooth on my skin. We are all watching the screen as he begins to glide the probe slowly, stopping every so often to adjust its angle. I hear Dr. Holder's fingers tapping at the computer keyboard, entering new data. He and Grant are focused only on the screen as I glance nervously from Samantha's image to Dr. Holder, trying to read his expression. No one is saying anything. Why isn't anyone saying anything?

I want to scream.

"Well, Stephanie," Dr. Holder breaks the unbearable silence, "Samantha looks wonderful. Everything looks very nice." I exhale. I look over at Grant who is smiling at the screen and my tears well up. "Please come back in a few months," requests Dr. Holder.

"Why?" I ask, confused. Does he need to check my insides again? Dr. Holder is wonderful but I was hoping we were done here.

"So we can meet your little Sam," he responds with a grin.

"Okay," I smile and sniff and as I blink, tears begin to stream. I take a long look at Samantha's image and predict that in five days, I will experience nothing short of a miracle. How does one prepare?

Four days later, after having done nothing to prepare, I receive a call from the hospital. They are expecting me the next day at 6:30 a.m. I'd been counting on there being certain advantages to having a scheduled labor and delivery date, namely that I would get the chance to shower, put on my wig and maybe a little waterproof mascara before we head out the front door. But 6:30 a.m. is causing my 'birth plan' to fade as I calculate how early I will have to arise in order to carry it out. Darn.

"Do you believe this is actually happening tomorrow?" I ask for about the hundredth time today as we sit down to dinner, our last with only two children. At that moment, Naomi swipes her plastic plate full of cut-up bananas and tofu hot dog off her tray and it clatters to the floor.

"Wow, *two* sisters for me soon, lucky me," Ethan responds, laughing, which gets a prideful smile out of Naomi. With lightning speed, Rio swoops in to eat up all that has fallen, and then sniffs around the floor for any hint of a crumb he might have missed. He then sits down next to Naomi, tail wagging, anxiously awaiting the next round.

"Oh Rio, my friend, your floor bounty could potentially double in a short while," I inform him, scratching behind his smooth, furry ear. "You're going to be one fat, happy dog."

I wake up the next morning to the phone ringing rather than my alarm clock beeping. It's hard to believe I slept at all considering what today is. I stayed up way too late last night, of course, puttering around the house, coming up with random small tasks to accomplish. I do this most evenings, but if purposeful procrastination were an Olympic event, last night I would have medaled.

"Hello?" I answer the phone groggily. I glance at the clock—5:26 a.m. My alarm is set to go off in four minutes.

"Mrs. Hosford? This is Huntington Memorial Hospital." I didn't know this hospital provides wakeup calls. What a great idea! "I see you're scheduled to come in at 6:30 but we have two emergency deliveries this morning so we'll need to push your induction back a few hours." Not a wakeup call.

"Oh, okay," I rasp, happy for possibly more sleep but also frustrated at the thought of anticipating Samantha's delivery for any longer. "This will happen today, though, right? My daughter's birthday will be May 18th?" I question nervously, grimacing at the thought of an alternate birth date and also because I probably sound like some sort of superstitious diva.

"You'll definitely be induced today," she answers. "We'll call you as soon as a bed opens up." I sigh, relieved. But now what?

I attempt to sleep a little longer but it's no use. I'm up. Up and anxious. No one else is awake yet, not even Grant, so I resume puttering. First, I check e-mail—reading, deleting and then dragging the chosen saved messages into their respective folders. Next, I check the refrigerator for expired items, though I find none because I perform this task often. What shall I do next? I could either begin to get ready for my life-changing event, *or* I could fold the rags in the laundry room and arrange them into piles based on color. I begin waddling toward the laundry room.

"What's up?" I hear Grant behind me. "Shouldn't you be getting dressed to go? Did someone call?" he asks.

"Oh yes. Sorry, hon, I didn't want to wake you before. It was the hospital earlier and they had emergencies and we've been pushed back to an unspecified time."

"Okay," Grant responds, going with the flow as usual, his internal schedule instantaneously realigned. "So are you going to tinker around here for a while then, maybe rear-range the bookcase?"

"Very funny," I retort, "and actually not a bad idea. I'll head there after I'm done with the rags."

Around 9:30 a.m., we receive the call. We're asked to arrive by 10:30. Extended suspense aside, these extra hours have been good. I've had time to shower, moisturize, put on my originally planned outfit, change into another one and then an even better one, make my bed, which always helps me think more clearly, and hug my children multiple times.

"We'd better head over there," Grant says at 10:10.

"Okay, kids, Mom and Dad have got to go," I tell them, holding out my hand for Ethan to help me up off the couch. "We love you very much. Be good for Grandma." I give them each an extra hug, Rio, too. Mom holds the door open for me. I bite my lip as I pause in front of her. She takes my hand and squeezes it.

"I love you," she tells me. "Call as soon as you have news."

"We'll be in touch," Grant says with a grin, gently pulling me toward the car.

"How are you?" he asks as we coast down our steep hill toward the freeway. "I'm good...mostly good." I long to feel all the way good, but I just can't seem to let it happen. It has only a little to do with the memories of childbirth that have been flashing through my head leaving me to feel uneasy about things like the IV that will have to be placed in my poor little dried out arm, and those opposite-of-sexy mesh underwear from the hospital that I will need to wear for a month, and the douching and the witch hazel pads on top of the enormous maxi-pad that will require constant chang-ing. Ugh. The bigger issue is my lingering uncertainty that any of this is possible in the first place.

Fear and Self-Doubt—the malicious twins that work together to put up roadblocks in front of our goals—have come back for a final showdown. It's like they've each grabbed one of my arms and are pulling me backward toward a precipice. Why can't they just let go of me so I can keep walking forward? Or is it me that needs to let go of *them*? I know what I need to do. But I need the right moment to make it happen.

Within minutes after checking in at the front desk of Labor and Delivery, we are ushered into a birthing room where I change into the 'fresh' hospital gown, hoist myself up onto the bed, and set my feet into the stirrups to await Dr. Mitchell.

"Oh, we have to tell the nurses that I am not allowed to breastfeed," I remind Grant in a moment of foresight and confidence in today's successful outcome. Stick with it, I plead with myself. This *will* happen today. Please be fine, Samantha. Both of us please be fine.

"Good morning," Dr. Mitchell says warmly, as he enters my suite, carrying a long, thin plastic stick with a small hook on the end of it. This is getting more real by the second. "How are you? Are you ready?" he asks. I look at Grant.

"I'm…we're ready," I answer, trying to hold my voice steady.

"I'm going to break the waters and start you on Pitocin. You'll most likely go into labor within an hour," Dr. Mitchell explains.

"Um, okay…and the epidural, when do I get that?"

"Don't worry, we'll get to you in time," replies one of the two nurses in the room, smiling. She's walking toward me with IV tubing and accessories. Oh crap, I really hate this part. I read her nametag. Mindy.

"Good luck with that, Mindy," I warn her, "I'm only

allowed to use my right arm for needles and my best veins are somewhat compromised right now."

"Don't worry, I'll find something," she says and takes my right arm, turning it every which way in search of something viable. "Here we go," she says, pointing to a place on the underside of my forearm next to my elbow. I see nothing.

"There's a vein there you can use?"

"Yes," she says. "Would you like to me to numb it up a bit with Lidocaine first?"

"Yes, please," I answer, still unconvinced as to the existence of this vein at all and imagining her digging painfully and fruitlessly around in my arm while I try not to scream or slap her or both. And yet, within a couple of minutes the area has been numbed, the IV placed and secured with tape.

"Nailed it," I tell her, impressed. "Thank you." But then I glance over at Dr. Mitchell waiting patiently with that hook.

Within a half hour of hook insertion and my waters breaking, which does not hurt, I begin to feel some contractions, which most definitely do hurt.

"Here they are," I wince. They increase rapidly in intensity and frequency. Oh Jeez. I take in a sharp breath, anticipating the next contraction. "Epidural please," I request as I attempt to remember some sort of helpful breathing for myself from the class Grant and I took almost seven years ago when I was pregnant with Ethan. They didn't work back then either.

The nurse pages the anesthesiologist. Is it supposed to be this quick? I had pictured being more in control, easing into this at a mellower pace. But I guess Samantha has other plans. Is she sensing her imminent freedom? I can't blame her one bit, as I would certainly want out of me, too, if I were Sam. Oh no, here comes another one.

I close my eyes and cling to the side rails, seeing only vast empty space with a few stars floating around in it. Shit, shit, shit, shit is all I can come up with in my head as my abdomen feels like it's being squeezed by King Kong. Let go, let go, let go.

Thankfully, the anesthesiologist arrives fairly quickly. I assume the fetal position, try to stay super still, and not think about my bare butt hanging out the rear of this robe. It's hard to believe I was stressed about the tiny nuisance in my arm less than an hour ago but here I am welcoming the mother of all needles being inserted into my back. I manage to smile at the anesthesiologist as the pain abates.

"Now who da man?" he asks.

"*You* da man," I respond without hesitating. "How many times do you get to hear that a day?" I ask him.

"Many," he says matter-of-factly. "That's why I took this job." He winks. And with that, he makes his exit.

Grant and I are alone in the room. I take a deep peaceful breath, now that I am not being consumed by acute pain. However, now I'm left to focus only on the enormity of what is about to happen.

"Babies are born every second, you know, so this is not a big deal," I announce to Grant.

"True," he answers, and by his tone I know he sees right through my attempt to deny the profound reality by which I am quickly becoming overwhelmed. He takes my hand and looks into my watering eyes.

"This is happening today, Steph. Samantha will be with us very soon. She is very real and she will be fine." I gaze at his earnest expression and then look up at the ceiling.

What is wrong with me? Will Samantha have to slap me in the face before I believe she really made it, that all of this happened? Is my mind trying to protect me from something? I'm tired of being protected. I'm tired of *thinking*. I want it to just happen and I want to be present. I notice that the lower half of my body is feeling really, really numb and to my surprise I don't like it.

Mindy enters the room, checks the various monitors and then my cervix.

"You're 7 cm dilated. I think it will go pretty quickly now," she says, removing her gloved hand from me.

"I don't feel a thing," I tell her. "I mean, *nothing*."

"Do you want to?" she asks.

"I…I think so…yes," I answer, confounded by my impromptu shift in disposition. All the chemo must have truly frazzled my brain.

"Let me call in Dr. Mitchell," she says. But she doesn't need to because he enters the room at that moment.

"Okay, I can turn off the epidural and come back in 20 minutes," he says after he is informed of my request.

"Good," I say, and then clasp my hand over my mouth in astonishment at my response. I look up at Grant. He smiles down at me.

"You can do this," he says. Dr. Mitchell flips a switch and the drugs cease. What if the pain is too much? Can I request to turn the medication back on and somehow not be seen as a pain in the ass? Doubtful.

But I want this. I *need* this, I realize now. My tendency toward denial can't be trusted. I need some authentic, irrefutable pain to help me shoo the ambiguity away and keep me connected to Samantha. This is our moment. I don't want a surreal experience. I want real.

It begins as a twinge. Oh, okay I can handle this. Then the twinges grow in size and number at supersonic speed, like in one of those films we watched in junior high where the scientist plants a seed and then the footage is sped up to witness the plant's entire life cycle within seconds. I'm back to my ineffective breathing techniques.

"Feeling it," I wince and call out to no one in particular. Dr. Mitchell reenters the room.

"Judging by your expression, I take it the epidural is wearing off," he says. I nod my head quickly. "Do you want me to turn it back on?" Yes.

"No," I hear myself say instead. It's more of a snarl, really. I'm sweating and gritting my teeth, but it's okay, it's good. The pain is giving me strength.

I think I'm beginning to understand the movie *Fight Club*.

"You're 10 cm dilated," Dr. Mitchell announces as he checks my cervix with a gloved hand. "Let's get ready to push."

"Is the epidural completely gone?" I ask, wondering if I am experiencing 'natural' childbirth and will hence have bragging rights to this.

"Close, but not completely. There wasn't enough time for that."

"Oh," I say, slightly disappointed. But then there's another contraction and I am thankful we ran out of time as my face contorts from the pain and my whole being is drenched in perspiration.

"When I tell you, you're going to push hard for 10 seconds and then stop," instructs Mindy. "Ready...push." Oh Jeez, okay. Take it easy. Don't pop blood vessels in your eyes or anything, I remind myself. I inhale deeply and then make a concerted effort to bear down while Mindy counts to ten. Can't she count any faster?

"Oh my God, this is hard. It hurts really bad," I cry when the first round ends.

"Here comes another one," Dr. Mitchell announces. Already?

"Deep breath, okay, push again. And one...two..." Mindy's voice drones on forever while I make a second attempt. "...and ten."

"Am I making any progress?" I ask, spent from those pushes.

"You are," Dr. Mitchell assures me from his front row seat on the rolling stool, "but we need a little more."

"Here's another," says Mindy. "Deep breaths. Let's go."

"You're doing great, Bug, almost there, I can see her," Grant encourages me. I go for another round, but she's not out yet. I'm exhausted. And I'm scared.

"One more time," requests Dr. Mitchell. It occurs to me that this baby is soon going to enter the world with or without my help. If I want to maintain my active role in the affair, then I need to make this happen now. But then I feel Doubt tug my arm again and hiss in my ear, "What if Samantha's not well? What if you did the wrong thing?" Fear tightens its grip, too, snickering, "This won't work. "What you're doing is insane." *Shut up, both of you!*

And then, from somewhere deep, I feel a swell of anger. Anger at everything I've given up on in the past when Fear and Doubt got in the way, from quitting ballet when I was twelve to not taking the MCAT in college to not going after jobs I really wanted because I was afraid of rejection or failure. Why didn't I believe in myself? I could have succeeded! I should have *tried*. And now this. I've come this far and yet those two still taunt me.

No. It's time to shut them up for good.

I'm not only going to succeed, but it's going to be great, glorious in fact. I believe it. For once, I believe it in every fiber of my being. Now I know who Grandma June was asking me to trust. Myself. *Trust yourself,* she meant. I do. *You're doing the right thing.* I am.

Now, fuck *off*! I wrestle free from their hold, turn around and shove those twin demons hard off the cliff with both hands. I watch them grasp for me futilely as they fall backward through the air.

"And...push now," commands Mindy. I look at Grant. He smiles and gives me a slight nod. I turn around from the cliff and step ahead onto solid ground. I close my eyes and gather up every last ounce of my strength, my resolve and the primal maternal longing that have all brought me to this point—and I push.

The physical pain I feel as Samantha rips through me and enters the world is both shocking and remarkable, as though she, too, has drawn upon a primordial instinct to break down any barrier on her way to emancipation. My world is in slow motion as Dr. Mitchell holds her tiny purple body, his huge hand cradling her wet head. And then time stops altogether. I grip the sides of the bed and all seems deafeningly silent as I wait an eternity for the sound that will release me from limbo.

"Waahh, weh, weh, waaahh" is music that starts my heart beating again.

I imagine Fear and Doubt in a crumpled lifeless heap at the foot of that tall cliff, and I smile wide.

I watch, fully in the moment, as Grant cuts the umbilical cord. Samantha is free. And so am I.

"You did it, Bug," says Grant, walking back up toward me. He takes my hand. "She's perfect."

"Aw, she has dimples," coos Mindy as she places the loosely wrapped bundle in my arms. I gaze down at her and shake my ski-capped bald head.

"And here you are," I say to Samantha, my finger gently stroking her pink cheek. I can think of nothing on my to-do list other than to stare at her for the next few decades. Our first journey together has ended. We are each on our own now, which for me is both liberating and peculiarly lonesome.

"Thank you," I rasp to Dr. Mitchell after he stitches me up. I hope someone's preparing an ice pack.

"You did wonderfully," he says. "You are a strong woman."

For once I simply accept the compliment and let myself feel an immense sense of pride.

The remainder of our 48-hour stay at the hospital is peaceful. Samantha performs splendidly on all of her initial newborn tests. Grant and Mom shuttle back and forth either to be with Samantha and me or at home with Ethan and Naomi. Both kids come to visit their new baby sister. Ethan holds Samantha so gently in the chair next to me while Naomi attempts to poke her repeatedly in the eye. I'm sure it's just an age thing…right?

Jenn visits, too, and gently rocks her niece. "You're awesome," she tells me.

"*You're* awesome," I insist back to her, remembering how she lifted me off Mom's kitchen floor last fall, when I was giving up on myself and aiming to schedule termination of the pregnancy.

We take some obligatory post-delivery pictures through-out my two-day recuperation and my wig manages to stay on straight for most of them. I don't wear the wig the whole time, but whenever it's off, I remember that I have four more rounds of chemo to get through and then radiation, so I stick it back on and try to forget. Although it pains me that I cannot breastfeed due to the toxins that could be in the breast milk, I am grateful that formula is available and I know Sam will be fine with it. She's most definitely survived worse.

Upon my discharge from the hospital I sit in the requisite wheelchair being maneuvered through the hallways by a teenage volunteer. I feel serene. Grant is holding Samantha in his arms. She is dressed in the tiniest of footie pajamas and a pink newborn ski cap with "Girl" embroidered on the front, just in case the pink doesn't clue people in.

The valet pulls up with our minivan, which I love and detest—love because it is a gift from my in-laws and fully paid for, and detest because it's a minivan and its appeal equates to the mesh underwear I have on. But here it is with two backward facing car seats and a booster strapped into it and as Grant gingerly puts Sam into her infant seat, it hits me.

Holy crap! We have *three* kids now. And two of them are very small and wear diapers. How in the world did I possibly think the tough part was over? I shake my head and take a very deep breath as I click my seatbelt into place.

And then I have a vision. I see the stick figures of my potential family I drew six months ago. The five of them leap off the paper and become real beings. Instead of standing together in a line, we walk down a path. Grant holds Naomi, I carry Samantha, and Ethan is between us. I don't recognize this path. It's not a place I've been before, but I know we're safe. There materializes a gauntlet of people, both living and not, who played a role in this part of our story—we pass by Mom, Jenn, Dad, Grandma June, my in-laws, Dr. Sung, Dr. Holder, even Drs. Hogan, Milbrook and Alford are there, among others—and they are all smiling, some nodding their heads and some are even clapping. I nod back at them as we stroll past. I know I'm still in this war for a while, but the most important battle has been won. The fight will continue, but now I'm armed with evidence of my capabilities.

"Honey," I say to Grant as we pull out of the hospital parking lot. I'm sitting behind him in the middle row with Samantha, gazing into her tranquil sleeping face, my hand on her tiny chest.

"Yeah, hon?" Grant answers.

"I think I'm ready to write about all this, just to share with our kids at some point, you know?" I see him smile toward the road ahead.

"Absolutely," he agrees.

"And I think I have a good title for it, too," I add.

Samantha stirs slightly as Grant turns on the radio and finds Michael Franti & Spearhead singing "Say Hey (I Love You)." Very nice.

We pull onto the freeway and head toward home.

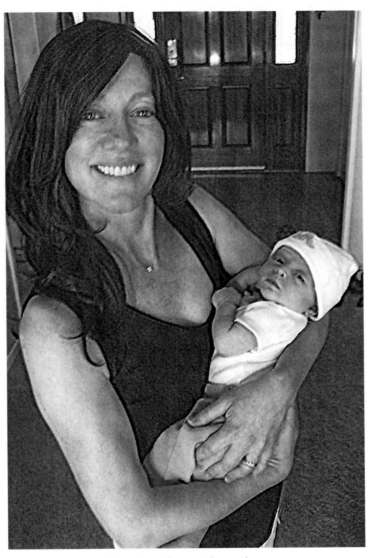

Newborn Samantha and me
(both of our bald heads covered fashionably)

October 2012
"Soul Meets Body" – Death Cab for Cutie

Dr. Sung is holding a printout of my test results. I let go of Grant's hand and sit up tall, the half-peeled bandage left dangling from my arm. My stomach is flip-flopping and my hands somehow manage to get even colder in this instant.

It's been five years since I received the call in the car from Dr. Wilson. Five years since discovering I was also pregnant. They say five years is a major milestone when it comes to surviving cancer. For the aggressive type I had, being cancer-free at three years was significant, but five is huge. Mostly, I've been living happily, striving to maintain a 'Zen' outlook on life. But it's always there, Cancer. Somewhere in the recesses of my mind, it's always there, smirking at me, daring me to get too confident in my victory. Cancer retained a sly power over me during these past few years. A stubborn cough could bring me to tears, a headache would keep me up at night fretting. I've been brought to my knees by a stomachache or a sore back, convinced that cancer had returned and that my body was riddled with it. I bite my lip and look at Dr. Sung expectantly.

She smiles widely. I wait an extra moment to exhale until I hear her say it.

"This is great!" she exclaims, waving the report and walking over to me. I finally let the air out of my lungs and then take in some more while I let this news sink in to my being. Dr. Sung gives me an enormous hug.

"This is really great news," she says now heading for the desk. Grant is next in line for hugs.

"I knew it," he whispers to me.

"Yes, you did," I whisper back, hugging him tightly. My muscles are relaxing all at once it seems, except for the ones in my face responsible for smiling.

"I'm hungry now," I giggle to him, flashing back to earlier this morning when my nerves made breakfast impossible for me to ingest.

Dr. Sung is sitting down, ready to jot some notes into my chart. "So who is your regular doctor?" she asks.

I pause. "Um, you?" I reply, confused.

"No, I mean, who do you see for other things, yearly checkups, a cold, that type of thing," she explains.

"Still you," I repeat.

She smiles. "I am going to see you only once a year now to check in," she says slowly, letting me ease into our breakup. "Unless of course you're experiencing any problems," she adds. I feel a wave of tension move through me at the thought.

Dr. Sung performs a short physical exam, feeling around my chest and armpits for anything suspicious. "It all looks and feels great," she says.

"I agree," adds Grant. I shake my head, roll my eyes and grin at him as I close my robe back up. The boobs do look good. After all, they *are* still fairly new, only three and half years old, with relatively low mileage, at least compared to the original ones.

The decision to get a double mastectomy came about following Sam's delivery and four more rounds of soul-sucking chemotherapy during which I almost threw in the towel and didn't finish because it was so vile and exhausting. I remember lying on our bed, unable to move following my second treatment and a painful injection of Neulasta.

"I'm done," I moaned to Mom. "I can't do this." But I did. I had to finish and know I did everything I could. Afterward, I had been given the choice of radiation or more surgery and upon learning of my chances of a second occurrence for each option, I chose the surgery. It was one of the hardest decisions of my life and the phone call I made to Dr. Santos to schedule it was gut wrenching. I think I dialed three times and hung up before I finally got the words "double mastectomy with reconstruction" out of my mouth. But each and every day, I look at my family and remember why I did it. It might have been aggressive, but I'd rather do too much than too little. And for me, it was the only way to truly help me move on.

"So what now?" I ask Dr. Sung.

"Now you go home and hug your beautiful children and I'll see you in a year," she replies. "How are Samantha, Naomi, and Ethan, by the way? Why didn't you bring them?" she asks as usual.

At some point during nearly every appointment over the last few years, Dr. Sung has requested I have the kids accompany me. And over the years, I've brought in each individually one time, praying on those days that I would not receive bad news in front of him or her. But that's been the extent of my efforts because aside from a visit to the cafeteria, this is not what I would consider Family Fun Day. So instead, as usual, Grant scrolls through some pictures of them on his phone while I dig through my wallet for their latest school and sports 2x3's.

"Oh, they are getting so big!" Dr. Sung expresses with her customary enthusiasm, "I love the girls' pony tails in this picture. And this one...are the girls the same size as each other now? They all look so happy. I bet Ethan is a wonderful big brother." I look on with her, grateful and still in awe that we all exist together. I would never claim that every moment of having three children has been pure bliss. There is plenty of fighting and screaming and claims of injustice occurring in the Hosford household, possibly even at this moment. Poor Grandma.

Is it really gone for good? The experts say that I now have less than a five percent chance of recurrence. I can live with those odds. I think the only way to get to zero percent is to die of something else first.

I've seen T-shirts and bumper stickers entreating me to 'Fuck Cancer' or 'Save the Tatas.' I understand the sentiment, but I'm partial to the 'Cancer Sucks' campaign — simple, true, not cavalier, not written by a teenage boy. All the same, regardless of the approach or slogan, what matters is continued research, early detection, and innovative treatment.

In the parking lot, Grant and I hold hands as we walk to the car, not the minivan (a.k.a. Red Rocket) but the fun one (a.k.a. Batmobile).

"Where should we go for lunch to celebrate?" Grant asks.

I ponder a moment. "Um, hmmm, maybe..." I hear my voice quiver on that last word. I burst into tears and my knees buckle. I would have collapsed onto the hot asphalt if Grant hadn't been holding my hand and caught me by the arm in time.

"Oh my God," I croak. "I wasn't expecting this."

"Just let it go, Bug," Grant says as he holds me up.

Five years of stress over this appointment was a lot to carry around, I suppose, despite all of the outlets I employed along the way—finally earning my black belt in taekwondo, completing a few more 5K's, 10K's and small triathlons. This was the finish line I wanted to cross most, and I can't stop the tidal wave of deliverance sweeping me along as I realize that I can finally stop running. So I simply let it.

A couple passes by, each person glancing over at us. The woman is wearing a pink scarf on her head and she looks away, uncomfortable, while the man offers me a look of empathy. I want to let them know that I am not sad, that these are happy tears, tears of relief. I want to share my success story with them and show them pictures of Samantha as proof that miracles can happen. Maybe hearing about our saga could help them get through theirs. But I say nothing and they continue walking toward the entrance.

I dab the corners of my eyes looking into the sunshade mirror in the car. I notice all of the laugh lines that fan out over my face. I think about how close I was to erasing those lines five years ago before my high school reunion. I've earned so many more since then. It would seem a shame now to cover up such hard work, so much evidence of happiness.

There was a time I wanted to forget everything from this era of my life, leave it behind me, focusing solely on the future. Now I know that not only is that impossible, but I don't *want* to forget.

Obviously, my daughters are hallmarks of the positives that came from my ordeal. The new boobs dwell in a sensation-free neutral zone as they are daily reminders of what was taken from me.

At the same time, I no longer need mammograms and

I'm able to fill out my clothes like never before. Even the purely negative aspects of my experience—the scars, the physical pain, the emotional upheaval, everything I went through—I want to keep.

Taken together, they remind me of when I was stronger than cancer, when I chose to go against convention and the majority opinion, when I persevered and didn't give up on myself or my family.

Someday my grandchildren will find a photo of me with my bald head and big round belly. They will be curious as to how that all came to be. I plan to tell them the story... personally.

My real life Party of Five

ACKNOWLEDGMENTS

Many are those who deserve my heartfelt thanks, but I would especially like to acknowledge my family. Grant—for being my husband and hero; Ethan, Naomi and Samantha—you are my sunshine (which is why I sing you three that song so much); Carol Abrams—my mom, for being consistently strong when you had every reason to fall apart; Jennifer Mucic—my sister and best friend, for propping me up time and time again; my in-laws, Shelby and Grant Hosford—for your unwavering support. Grandma June—thanks for the visit. I would also like to recognize my team of doctors at City of Hope and elsewhere. Thank you for stepping up to handle my unique case and for guiding me through it with such care and expertise. Thank you to the wonderful team at Nothing But The Truth Publishing—you are the perfect fit for me. Finally, a huge thank you to all my friends who supported me through everything, from diagnosis to book completion, and all the milestones in between.

CPSIA information can be obtained at www.ICGtesting.com
Printed in the USA
BVOW04s1533090615

403850BV00003B/215/P